AMAZING AUDITION

An exciting anthology of stories
about Liverpool legend Billy Fury,
whose life and music has affected
people in so many ways

ISBN 978-1-78222-831-8

Book design, layout and production management by Into Print
www.intoprint.net, +44 (0)1604 832140

Contents

Foreword

Welcome to this book on behalf of myself and the Co-Authors. Every story is based on Liverpool legend Billy Fury whose life and music has affected people in so many ways. I have listed the stories in alphabetical order of the first names, having decided against deciding an order of importance. Every one of the stories is the most important one to the writer and to me.

Obtaining stories and putting them into my desired format has only been achieved by many Facebook messages, Emails, telephone conversations, research and letters. Every finalised story has been approved by the author and I am impressed with the interest level and diversity of the contributions.

I apologise for the quality of some of the pictures which in some cases are copies of crumpled originals.

The term Rock n Roll appears frequently in the stories and there are various ways of printing it. I have decided use Rock n Roll throughout the book to achieve uniformity.

Acknowledgements

Editor Jenny Green   She does a fantastic job for me and for you, the reader in correcting my grammar and spelling in addition to advice and general encouragement

The Co-Authors   For their stories, patience and co-operation when I have requested more information

Lee Fry   For pictures he has supplied and advice on other pictures

Chris Eley   He has supplied pictures, information and help on many occasions and has gone to enormous lengths to provide his story

My Wife, Joan   Constant advice, help, proof checking and for her story

Publishers   Anne and Mark Webb of Paragon Publishing,

To everyone who has helped while I have been producing this book

Thank you to Lee Fry for the use of your copyright picture and for the picture of Billy with his 'mobile phone' on the back cover

1: MICHAEL PARKINSON

There are many conflicting versions of the Billy Fury audition story, after doing a lot of research, this is mine.

In May 1958 Ron recorded six demo tracks of himself performing songs he had written himself on a 78 rpm acetate record. This was in a small room behind the shop that the Percy Phillips family owned at 38 Kensington, Liverpool. Ron sent a picture of himself and a tape of the songs to impresario Larry Parnes but did not get a reply. His mother wrote again to Parnes who this time replied, Larry invited Ron to see him at the Birkenhead Essoldo on 1 October 1958. One of his shows 'The Larry Parnes Extravaganza' was being staged that night. One aspect of the story that has become clear to me is the role of Larry Parnes. I believe that he decided exactly what he planned to do after listening to the tape that Ron had sent to him. Although Larry did not normally attend all his shows, he made an exception in going to Liverpool because he wanted to see and hear Ron perform before putting his plan into action.

In November 2011 I videoed Vince Eager who was one of the performers in the Extravaganza show describing meeting young Ronnie at the stage door and what happened next. I loaded this to my YouTube channel *Michael notthatone Parkinson* with the title *'Billy Fury by Vince Eager, Audition at Birkenhead Essoldo.'* Vince said, I was walking out of the stage door to get a snack from a Wimpy Bar when I bumped into a young man who was wearing a gaberdine coat with the collar turned right up looking very much like a cross between Elvis Presley and James Dean, a very good looking guy. He appeared to be very shy and asked me in a very broad scouse accent if Mr Parnes was in the theatre, Larry Parnes was the manager for Tommy Steele, Marty Wilde and myself at that time. I said that he was but can I tell him who is looking for him, the man said my name is Ronald Wycherley and I've sent him a tape of some songs I have written and I'd like to know if he has listened to them. So I went into the theatre and mentioned this to Larry and he said well fetch him in so I went out and said to Ron that Mr Parnes is in and he would like to see you.

We went into the dressing room that Marty and I were sharing. I introduced

Ronnie to Larry and from then on Larry did all the talking and it finished up that Larry invited Ronnie to sing a song so although he had brought a guitar with him he borrowed the Hofner Committee guitar belonging to Kenny Packwood who was the guitarist for Marty Wilde. Ronnie sang 'Maybe Tomorrow'. He was very good looking, very sensual and very photogenic and we all stood there in amazement, the thing was that in those days very few singers, if any, wrote their own songs, 90% of them came from America, Nobody at this time had written their own song, recorded it and had a hit. Then he sang 'Margo'. There were girls outside the theatre who were always there before our shows, they heard the songs and were screaming with delight at what they heard. Larry decided that the reaction of the girls was way above normal, he looked at Ronnie and said, would you like to go on the show tonight? Ronnie was taken aback but agreed.

He was introduced by another young man who was making his first appearance, that was Jimmy Tarbuck, who was also being auditioned that night, so there were two future greats, one introducing the other. Billy was there when the curtains opened, he looked great and once again borrowed Kenny's guitar though there was a band behind him, the John Barry Seven. He sang 'Maybe Tomorrow' 'Margo', and 'Don't Knock Upon My Door'. Ron said later that his knees were literally knocking together but the fans thought it part of the act. The audience loved his performance and the girls loved his appearance.

Then what happened was that Larry obviously decided that Ronnie was something special, he had already given him the name Billy Fury (there are stories that he didn't but he did). At the end of the show Larry signed him on and told him that he wanted him to appear the very next night at the Manchester Stretford Essoldo. Ron's parents could not believe it when he got home and told them what had happened. The next morning he was packing his suitcase to go to Manchester and his mother said that she was worried about him going off on his own. Ron convinced her that it was the best chance that he would ever have.

The following day we picked Billy up at a bus stop, his brother Albie was there to see him off and Billy got in with his suitcase. That night he went on the stage as Billy Fury, there was a big sign in the foyer saying, 'Welcome to the new teenage rage Billy Fury'. He went on, he stole the show, he was absolutely brilliant, this time John Barry did play some of the backing for him. We stayed that night at the Midland Hotel in Manchester and the following day we all flew to London, it was not a very good flight for Billy because he was using the little brown bag all the time. On arrival in London we were taken to Larry's apartment, where I lived, Billy and I finished up being flatmates.

I am very grateful that Vince came over to my house for me to video this story (he only lives four miles away) but I am sure that he did not realise that Larry Parnes had already formulated his plan. When Ron sang those songs it confirmed what Larry had decided. So, whilst it was a total surprise to Ron that Larry asked him to go on stage in the second half of the show it was an example of how clever Larry Parnes was.

The only thing in Ron's mind was to sing the songs, he had written himself, to Marty Wilde in the hope that Marty would sing and record them. The sincere and unselfish reaction of Marty Wilde is conveyed in his story, Chapter 22.

A young looking Billy Fury. Picture copyright Lee Fry

2: BILLY FURY DANCE – NOTTINGHAM ARTS THEATRE

One Sunday afternoon in March 2009 my wife Joan and I were driving near Nottingham, when Paul Robey on BBC Radio Nottingham announced a Billy Fury song. Joan jumped about with enjoyment as it was being broadcast because she is an ardent Billy Fury fan. Paul Robey is Joan's favourite presenter who has a Sunday afternoon slot which he refers to as 'nostalgia and nonsense'. I had arranged for Phil Kelsall, principal organist of the Blackpool Tower Ballroom, to perform an afternoon concert at Nottingham Arts Theatre in July of the following year. For an additional eighty pounds I knew that I could put an evening show on as well. I had long believed that the songs of Billy Fury were suited to routines by dancers so I thought about putting a Billy Fury Dance Show together. I mulled over the idea and had two obstacles. One was that some of Billy Fury's backing group, the Tornados, were currently performing a show called Halfway to Paradise – The Billy Fury Story, I did not want to risk them complaining so contacted Chris Raynor (one of the Tornados who lives near Nottingham). I explained my idea asking if he had any objection. He assured me that he thought it was a great idea and said that he and his wife would want to come to the show. I then asked him about my other worry which was 'would I get permission from the owners of Billy's recordings to use them in my show?' Chris's reply was not what I wanted to hear. He said, 'if you ask the people in London they may say no so it is better not to ask and just do it'. I thanked Chris for his input but made a mental note that I would not consider doing the show without getting permission to use the recordings.

After much investigation I discovered that most of the tracks were owned by Universal Music and some Parlophone recordings by Lisa Voice who had been Billy's partner for a number of years. I contacted Paul Veitch who is Head of Creative Licensing at Universal Music London. He gave me permission to use the tracks owned by them provided that the Theatre had a Performing Rights Society license. After more work I got permission from Lisa Voice to use the tracks that she owned. That was the easy bit accomplished, my next objective was to write a script (something I had never done before). It was easy to obtain information about Billy Fury and I had soon downloaded loads from the internet. Putting it together in a show format and deciding which songs to use was a huge challenge. Joan had many Billy Fury recordings but by no means all. I started to put something together but lacked inspiration so decided to go to the grave of Billy Fury in the hope that it would trigger creativity. Looking back, it was a strange idea that paid great dividends.

On 26 August 2009 I went to Westminster Paddington Cemetery at Mill Hill in North London and asked a groundsman where the grave of Billy Fury was. He replied 'I am asked that question nearly every day and it is the most visited and best maintained grave in the whole cemetery'. It transpired that he was the Head Groundsman and was going that way so escorted me to the grave. On arrival, there was a man sitting on a wooden bench and a lady kneeling down tending to the grave. I explained the reason for my visit to the man who said, 'you should speak to her, she is Billy's number one fan'. The lady looked at me and said, 'just one of many'. The lady was Marina Weedon and the man on the bench was Paul her ex husband who is a taxi driver. They were divorced but once a month he took her from her home in Chiswick to look after the grave. Marina told me that there were two Billy Fury fan clubs. She was in one called The Sound of Fury, and she suggested that I speak to a man called Chris Eley at that club. Paul was in the newer one called 'Billy Fury In Thoughts of You' and my contact there would be Mags Cummings. *(I understand that this club has now closed down)* The fact that one of them was in each club meant that they shared information from both clubs.

Marina told me a story; When she was 16 her Father bought her an expensive watch for her birthday present. Her elder sister took her to a Billy Fury Show at the Southall Dominion Theatre in April 1962 as her treat. Marina was captivated by Billy's performance. She joined the other girls screaming with delight and throwing her arms in the air. At the end of the show she realised that the watch was missing, perhaps it had shot off her wrist. She and her sister searched for a long time but could not find it. Not only were they late home but Marina had to tell her Father that the watch was lost. He was annoyed and vowed never to buy her another one. After Marina and Paul had gone I made a note of the words inscribed on the headstone which were:-

IN LOVING MEMORY OF

RONALD WYCHERLEY

(BILLY FURY)

PASSED AWAY 28TH JANUARY 1983

AGE 42

SADLY MOURNED BY LISA, PARENTS,

RELATIVES AND FRIENDS

HIS MUSIC GAVE PLEASURE TO MILLIONS

REST IN PEACE DARLING BILLY

I decided to use the words 'His music **still** gives pleasure to Millions' in my script because there I was, twenty six years later, and people were still enjoying his music.

(My later investigation revealed that the Sound of Fury Fan Club arranges for regular professional annual cleaning and any necessary repairs to the grave, on behalf of the Billy Fury Estate, Ms Lisa Voice and that Marina does a regular general tidy up also on behalf of the Sound of Fury).

The following evening I contacted Chris Eley and told him of my plan. He was enthusiastic and promised to send CDs of all the Billy Fury recordings. True to his word over the next few days various CDs, information and pictures dropped through my letter box. Joan and I found the task of deciding which songs to use in the show time consuming but enjoyable. After much deliberation we decided on the songs. I decided on a format of some narration telling the Billy Fury Story interspersed with songs and choreographed dance of varied tempo. I broke this down into scenes of around twelve minutes per scene.

This is a list of songs which finally **made it into the script:-**

Give me your word
Do you really love me too
Please love me
Margo don't go
Maybe tomorrow
Don't knock upon my door
It's only make believe

We were meant for each other
I'd never find another you
I love how you love me
Once upon a dream
Gonna type a letter
Running around
I'll show you
Last night was made for love
In my room
Collette
Wondrous place
Like I've never been gone
Jealousy
Because of love
Lady
King for tonight
Stand by me
How many nights, how many days
Run to my loving arms
In thoughts of you
I'll never fall in love again
In summer
Turn my back on you
Letter full of tears
Forget him
I will
I'm lost without you
Devil or Angel
I'll never quite get over you
Somebody else's girl
A thousand stars
Halfway to paradise

In addition to the songs I included a special scene where the cast sang the 23rd psalm, Billy reading a poem that he had written himself and 'Sweet Jessica' a reference to my chosen charity Jessie's Fund.

I continued to work on script writing and at the same time exercised my mind on how I would get dancers and narrators to perform in the show. I was not getting on well with this until November 2009 when dame fortune smiled on me. I went to a small dance show in a studio at the Nottingham Arts Theatre. I thought it would be a good opportunity to meet dancers. Maggie Andrew appeared to be in charge and I spoke to her about my plans. I had met Maggie four years previously when I had collaborated with the London Studio Centre in putting on three performances of 'Oh What a Lovely War' at the Nottingham Arts Theatre. Maggie had done 'front of house' and told me how much she had enjoyed the shows every time I had seen her since. Maggie offered to direct my Billy Fury Dance Show for me and I accepted her offer, she wrote these words in a confirmation email to me a couple of days later:-

'Could we meet for coffee this week and I will tell you all about me and what I think I could bring to the show in terms of help etc. I am anxious that you will see that it is my love of theatre etc that motivates me. I think it is important that we get it out there as soon as possible to dancers, they get really busy! Maggie'.

I accepted Maggie's suggestion and we agreed a deal. Maggie had directed a few youth group productions at the Arts Theatre and had contact with many young performers in the Nottingham area. We organised an application form and circulated it to various dance schools, drama and theatre groups. We set up and I negotiated payments to the Arts Theatre for rehearsals. There is a lot of boring, expensive, but necessary stuff to do in promoting a show like theatre hire contracts and insurance for instance. Maggie had a close relationship with the Nottingham Post and BBC Radio Nottingham and they helped by giving publicity involving details of the show and the dancers that we wanted. It was decided that there would be one performance on Sunday evening 11 July 2010, the day that Phil Kelsall played his concert in the afternoon. It was then that Maggie pointed out to me that I had caused her a huge problem. She wanted all of the theatre for the whole day of the show but was not able to have it because Phil was arriving at around 12 noon and had to get theTechnics organ on stage and set up for his performance at 2pm. It was rather a strange situation because if I had not been putting the Phil Kelsall concert on the Billy Fury Show would not have happened.

Many dancers applied to take part in the show but the first audition had to be cancelled on the day because of heavy snowfall. Another audition was arranged (more expense) and we finished with 32 performers, mostly dancers but some would do narration as well and some of the dancers would assist Maggie by choreographing routines. I had to book and pay for many rehearsals. Maggie had banned me from attending rehearsals but, to my surprise, invited Joan and I to go into the theatre studio for a preview that she had arranged for us. I was impressed that the combination of Billy's songs, narration and dance worked beautifully. After the preview Maggie told me her reason for putting it on. She wanted me to pay for the theatre for another performance the day after the original Sunday night show. I thought, 'more expense' but agreed so a further performance was booked making a two night show. I had invited Jean Wycherley (Billy's Mother) to the show but had not received a reply. Maggie and the girls composed a letter to her which they all signed. This is exactly what the letter said:-

Dear Mrs Wycherley

We are writing to invite you to an event we are putting on honouring Billy Fury's memory. Although Michael Parkinson has already contacted you regarding our performances on the 11th and 12th of July 2010. We thought it would be beneficial to hear from us exactly why we are involved with this project.

The Billy Fury Show is being performed at the Nottingham Arts Theatre with all proceeds going to a charity called Jessie's Fund. Originally it was a one night charity event but tickets went so fast we felt we needed to add another night to be able to spread Billy's music further. All the dances are being choreographed to his music and we loved it so much we felt the need to inspire others with it as well. We have thirty two girls dancing throughout the show. Some of us being responsible for the choreography also.The age range of the girls is between ten and twenty five although the majority are between thirteen and sixteen.

We hope you can attend, however even if you can't we wanted to let you know how much we've enjoyed being allowed to use both Billy Fury's music and clips from his films to be able to tell his life story through dance and narration.

Yours faithfully
Maggie Andrew (and signatures of all the girls)

Maggie was proud to tell me a few day's later that Jean wanted to come and that John and Mags Cummings (of the 'In Thoughts of You' fan club were going to bring her). Maggie found additional inexpensive rehearsal space about four miles from Nottingham at the Patricia James dance studio in Carlton so many of the girls travelled out there. I was welcomed to one of them. One of the difficulties that Maggie and I endured was the constant demand for rehearsals causing my costs to escalate well above what I had anticipated. Maggie never had all the girls together at a rehearsal until the day of the performance. Although they were only young performers they all had huge demands on their time.

I included these tributes to Billy Fury in the programme and printed them exactly as they were sent to me with no editing:-

From Mags Cummings of the Billy Fury In Thoughts of You Fan Club

I first met Billy at Manchester Hippodrome when I was fifteen and was hooked. I was fortunate in getting to meet him many times and eventually became a friend. One of my first encounters at the age of sixteen was when I slid under a locked gate at Buxton Pavilion Gardens where Billy was waiting in his car whilst his manager had gone to find someone to allow them out. I'd given Billy a birthday cake during the show and when I approached the car he mentioned it and then motioned for me to come closer and gave me my first 'proper' kiss. He was a lovely gentle man. A complete contrast to his electric persona on stage. It was a very sad day indeed when he was prematurely taken from us.

From Alvin Stardust

I first met Billy Fury when I was a teenager. It was the first tour I'd ever done with my band The Fentones.

As soon as Bill came on stage at the soundcheck it was obvious he was 'A STAR'. Only a couple of times in my life in the music business have I had that feeling. Elvis, The Beatles, Buddy Holly and maybe a couple more. Not bad company eh?

Often we shared dressing rooms and we became good friends. He was a great bloke and a fantastic natural performer. A great loss to us all when we lost him. But his memory lives on alongside his fabulous recordings.

Very sincerely Alvin Stardust

From Chris Eley – The Sound of Fury-Official Billy Fury Fan Club

When I was first approached by Michael Parkinson and informed of his intention to stage a tribute in song, story and dance to the late great Billy Fury, my first impression was 'How original and refreshing'. That perception has not changed, because indeed this is the first time such a show has been produced without the use of singers. Tribute acts do a sterling job in promoting Billy's legacy but this really does promise something different. Since having the privilege of becoming involved in the project I have become aware of just how sincere Michael is in this venture-both in his love of Billy's music and in his dedication to Jessie's Fund, which is about helping children with special needs and which he has been supporting for about eight years now. Choosing songs for the performances from among the wonderful three hundred or so numbers recorded across several labels from 1958-83 has not been an easy task, and whilst the show is based primarily on most of his hit singles, a few of the other less well known but equally valid, some might say better tracks, found on B sides, albums, EPs and even from the inexplicably chart-barren Parlophone, or wilderness years, have been included. Were the show able to be longer the diversity of Billy's wonderful output would have been further displayed. Because of the charity aspect of the show Universal/Decca and Ms Lisa Voice of the Billy Fury Estate have kindly consented for the wonderful selection of tracks you will hear, to be played as indeed have the owners of various clips and photos you will experience during the show. Best of all, in addition to promoting surely some of the finest popular music ever to be recorded, your participation by attending this event will be helping a very good cause, named Jessie's Fund.

We lost what many feel was Britain's finest performer of his era and genre all too soon on 28 January 1983, when Billy finally lost his battle against the heart valve problem that had dogged him since his childhood. Since then his fans have maintained and enhanced his grave at Mill Hill in London, placed a lectern in Liverpool Anglican Cathedral, held tribute weekends nearly every year, placed a bronze statue at the Liverpool pier head, and worked with music companies on various vinyl and CD releases. Various tribute acts and bands have appeared, with many of the best remaining on the circuit today, and three Billy acts have appeared on 'Stars in their Eyes' over the years. In 1998 an excellent Omnibus TV documentary was screened, bringing back many fans to the fold. In 2008 Billy, who has two fan clubs in the UK and an excellent independent website, enjoyed the incredible feat for a 'Retro' artist in achieving a top 10 DVD (re-entry from 2007) and a Top 10 CD. Together with Dusty Springfield, Billy is the most requested (and played) solo artist on Brian Matthews long running Sounds of the 60's BBC 2 radio show. 'Forget Him' – not likely! This tribute in song and dance has been produced with a high level of integrity and genuine resolve and provides a rare opportunity to hear the original 'Sound of Billy Fury' on a theatre stage. So sit back and enjoy the musical legendary Billy Fury, presented in a unique, tasteful and enjoyable way.

Chris Eley

A few days before the concerts were to take place I was driving near to where Maggie lives and saw her walking along the pavement so stopped and got out of the car to speak to her. To my dismay she was distraught and threw her arms around me and between tears told me that it was not going to happen as there were so many problems. She calmed down after we had spoken for a few minutes and I was able to reassure her about a few things. The incident may have helped Maggie but left me worried about what would happen on the first night.

When the big day dawned Maggie, technical staff and others were in the theatre at 7am and got to work on the technical and dress rehearsal. When Phil Kelsall arrived, at around 12 noon for his 2pm concert the stage had to be allocated to him. The technical crew helped him get the organ on stage and speakers set up. He had got up early that morning to collect the trailer that he hires to transport the organ and travelled to Nottingham from Blackpool. He was not allocated a dressing room because they were all occupied by dancers so just before the audience were allowed into the theatre Phil (who had just been awarded the MBE) and myself had to get changed at the back of the stage. Phil was not happy and I can distinctly remember his words 'I have performed in Church Halls that are better organised than this place'. I felt guilty because it was my fault in arranging two shows in one day and not the fault of the Arts Theatre. His performance went well as usual and the audience departed leaving Maggie with sole control of the theatre for the remainder of the day.

There was just one parking space near the front of the theatre and I wanted to make sure that this was saved for Mags and John Cummings when they arrived with Jean Wycherley. I borrowed four white painted wrought iron chairs and table from the coffee bar and situated them on the road in the parking space which Joan, myself Linda Shawley and Chris Eley sat on until Mags and John Cummings arrived with our special guest. This caused much laughter amongst early arrivals and passers by so we all started to enjoy ourselves. Many bus and car drivers gave us a hoot and a wave, it was great fun. When Jean arrived we took the chairs back into the theatre and I went on to my role of selling programmes inside. Someone came to me and suggested that I should go outside and give a programme to Jean which I did. Unknown to me, my friend, whose YouTube name is catman2007, had set it up and was videoing. It is still on his YouTube Channel with the simple heading *Mrs Jean Wycherley*. She can be seen standing and chatting with Billy Fury fans who had come to the show before I gave her a programme. The performance was brilliant but poor Maggie did have her problems because amongst other things one of the girls was sick at the back of the stage whilst one of the numbers was being performed. It was a full house and everyone enjoyed the show. At the end Chris Eley presented pictures of Billy to Jean Wycherley, Joan and myself. The picture that we received featured Billy Fury and these words:-

This endearing picture of Billy Fury from the mid sixties is presented to Michael and Joan Parkinson in recognition of their promotion of the musical legacy of Billy. In coupling a varied selection of recordings from Billy's entire career output, with dance, they have created a unique show in laudable support of Jessie's Fund. With grateful thanks Chris, Linda and the team of The Sound of Fury (Official Billy Fury Fan Club)
Nottingham – 11th July 2010

A surprising thing happened after the show whilst the presentations were being made and all the dancers were on stage with the curtain closed. My wife, Joan who is very shy and had never made a speech before in her life suddenly said that she wanted to speak to the performers, she said, 'That was the most fabulous thing I have ever seen, you all did really well and I really enjoyed it'. The feedback that I received through this and subsequent Billy Fury Shows is that the young people involved like the Billy Fury songs and enjoy dancing to them and I hear the same comment over and over again. The audience loved listening to the Billy Fury recordings coupled with the dance routines. The show was performed again the following night, everyone was more relaxed this time and even director Maggie Andrew could enjoy it.

A few days after the shows Chris Eley sent me his review, it is rather long but I include it here because it gives a good explanation of the show:-

During the afternoon we were treated to a performance, for Jessie's Fund, by Phil Kelsall MBE, the lead organist from the Blackpool Tower Ballroom. The venue was well attended and the performance magnificent, as might be expected, and very well received by Phil's fans. During the early evening Billy's Mum arrived (Michael had been sitting on a theatre chair in the road saving her a parking space – told you he had humour!). She was actually brought along by a very nice couple, John and Mags Cummings, the latter of course from Billy Fury in Thoughts of You Fan Club team. It was great to see Jean again and as always her presence was to add greatly to the event. Mags and I were allowed in for a little while to take photos of the girls who would be performing for us shortly afterwards. This was because taking photos during the performance may have been off-putting for the girls, although no doubt some proud parents did snap away. What was outstanding whilst talking to the girls, aged from about nine to early twenties was that they now loved the music of Billy Fury; an artist even most of the parents didn't know about. That said they were going round singing his songs. This was so heartening and the photo shows them yelling out Billy Fury and punching the air when I asked them to say his name for the photo. Their enthusiasm and infectious sense of fun boded well for the performance and we were not to be disappointed. During act one we were treated to a mixture of narrations of Billy's life, mostly well delivered indeed and never less than competent throughout the show, and nineteen songs in the first act, beginning with *Give me Your Word* and ending with *Like Iv'e Never Been Gone*. The narrations were rendered even more effective by the well known Halfway to Paradise picture of Billy kneeling with his guitar which Michael had had extended, illuminated and positioned at the side of the stage. Every number was different in approach and each was highly enjoyable, with many novel twists throughout the whole evening. The girls, of whatever age, danced their hearts out for us and it was such a wonderfully innocent show, quite the opposite to what I envisaged until I met the girls in rehearsal. Prior to attending I had thought of sexily dressed over sixteen year olds, pouting and go-go dancing raunchily 60's style (wishful thinking I guess!). I had been looking forward to Billy's sensuality being somehow transferred to dancing girls-a sort of reversed erotic effect yet demonstrating his highly sexualised image. However, this unexpected combination of ages and dance styles, (which was down to the show director) coupled with the innocence and cheeriness actually worked on a very different level was, perhaps as it should be for such a fund, highly wholesome; although this is not to say that there were not attractive girls on stage. To hear recordings of such numbers as *Please Love Me* and others not normally performed by tribute acts, played in public for the first time was terrific. Difficult to pick out individual routines but *Gonna Type a Letter* was perhaps the major show highlight. With its office setting, a sub plot and a lot of movement including tap dancing, it really was great fun. *I'll Show You* was the total opposite, nicely done and the gold ponchos were a lovely touch; *In My Room* was highly poignant and the idea of having 'French' striped tops for *Collette* was clever. The dancing combined somersaults, tap dancing, twist, jive and various other styles and it was a credit to the girls and their marvellous stage manager, Maggie Andrew, and there was not an obvious falter or mis-step in either act-they had worked, and been worked that hard. For an amateur production, with some girls who had never been on stage before it was incredible. It would be unfair to single out any individual but one must be, albeit for a different reason. Lauren Pringle, a young cast member had been working so hard for weeks but was taken ill during the final rehearsal and so missed the show. We really felt for her, and her family and friends and hope she is now fine. The show also featured projected images of Billy on a big screen and being the anorak that I am had to tell Michael that some of the images were reversed and will need changing for any future shows. Also Billy did not cut the *One and only* in 1980 but in 1982, wonder how I missed that, but these are only very minor constructive criticisms for what was a great show.

Act 2 followed the pattern of narration and dance and opened with a great tango scene for *Jealousy,* the girls stunning in all Red and Black dresses, setting the tone for the rest of the act. *Because of love* featured a hula style dance, quite neat and I am sure *Lady* impressed Billy's Mum. *King for Tonight* had a great ending as did several others, how the girls could get into some of the tableaux positions they did beats me, and the delight and exuberance was there especially during *How Many Nights, How Many Days.* I made a note, gymnastics amazing but I cannot recall exactly which numbers featured it, great stuff anyway. *In Summer* was, as it should be, very bright and happy-these girls never stopped smiling, *Turn My Back On You* really rocked away with two older girls jiving, and the postman's hat was a nice touch during *Letter Full of Tears.* Quite how the girls managed such rapid costume changes I don't know and whoever provided the costumes needs a major thank you. Having very young girls in the show allows for cute-and this was typified by a brilliant *Devil or Angel* where the 'imps' appeared behind a barrier with devils ears on and were joined by Angels for a mock encounter-clever stuff, and so well performed. Great ideas from Maggie, such a talented and professional director, as well as a lovely warm person. Her genuine love for 'her girls' and a fierce protectiveness bear testament to this. *Halfway to Paradise* inevitably closed the Billy part of the show, and there had been really poignant moments, especially during scene eleven which combined Psalm 23, poetry by Billy (from *Paper Aeroplanes)* and *Forget Him* but the performance of *Sweet Jessica* which closed the show was both highly poignant and truly beautiful. The girls sung the tribute to Jessica with a lovely acoustic guitar backing and some solo verses. Unfortunately the girl who played the guitar injured her hand and could not play on stage, which would have added even more pathos to the number. I did say there was such a lot of talent involved in this production and that is an understatement, from the writer, through producer and assistant, the cast, technicians and the theatre staff, a very professional and wonderfully enjoyable production. What I know about dancing you could write on a match-box-but I know what I saw and it was splendid. In addition to supporting the excellent fund it gave Billy's musical legacy a great uplift and crossed generations, which is what we need to do. A total of forty of Billy's songs were used, mostly hits but mixed with other Decca, Parlophone and Polydor tracks in an excellent mix. One more act would have meant even more varied songs, but two acts was about right. The detailed programme contained personal tributes from Vince Eager, Alvin Stardust and notes from both fan clubs, plus full credits.

To round off the evening Billy's Mum received a presentation photograph of Billy from the cast all involved in the production, and a signed photo list of the cast. Then Michael and Joan received a presentation, with gratitude for promoting Billy so positively. from the Sound of Fury and on behalf of Billy's fans everywhere. Linda and I would like to thank Michael and his wife Joan, a massive Billy fan, for their courtesy and friendship. Michael thanked the fans who attended and we in both fan clubs would echo that without such support all this talent and work would have been wasted. Without the original idea and script of course nothing would have happened, so thanks Michael and Joan, from us all and Billy, who would I am sure be as usual, bemused at the fuss, but chuffed to bits.

Chris Eley (*Sound of Fury Fan Club*)

Whilst I was pleased with the audience reaction and this review I was aware that some of the narration was not clearly audible to the whole of the audience and knew that I would improve it for subsequent shows. Chris was too modest to point out that it was he who donated the framed pictures. Director, Maggie Andrew lived that show and though she demanded high standards from the performers they liked and respected her. The Father of one of the performers videoed the show, I have used it to load many of the dance routines to YouTube and list just three of them here:-

Billy Fury Dance, Lady, Nottingham Arts Theatre
Billy Fury Dance, How Many Nights, Nottingham Arts Theatre
Billy Fury Dance, Gonna Type a Letter, Nottingham Arts Theatre

The performers had made a collection and presented a bottle of champagne to Joan and I with a note thanking us for giving them an opportunity to perform in a wonderful show.

As a result of the shows I donated £1246 to Children's Music Therapy Charity Jessie's Fund. The figure included members of the cast donating travelling expenses and costume makers donating fees that I had offered, another example of the lovely attitude of people in amateur theatre.

The Performers were:-

Lauren Banks
Helen Belcher
Alice Bentham
Holly Cuffley
Vikki Dixon
Frankie Farish
Skye Fletcher
Zoe Garton
Helen Greatorex
Jasmine Hardy
Hania Hickling
Megan Hill
Imogen Jesson
Erin Keogh
Emily Kirk
Charlotte Lawley
Fabiane Leame
Amy Pickance
Lauren Pringle
Chloe Richardson
Sarah Robinson
Alice Sikora-Bradley
Amanda Tate
Paige Taylor
Lily Taylor-Ward
Faith Tucker
Cora Vanaman
Pippa Waite
Isabella Walker
Kirsty Walton
Lizzy Whynes
Laura Wilbraham

Joan, Myself and Linda Shawley reserving a parking space for Jean Wycherley

Jean with young dancer Fabiane Leame after the show

Mags Cummings watches as Chris Eley presents a picture to Joan and I

Performers blowing kisses to Chris as he took the photograph

3: BILLY FURY DANCE – LYTHAM ST ANNES, BLACKPOOL

After the success of my Billy Fury Dance Show at Nottingham I wanted to put the show on at other venues and had learned a few lessons. I decided to change the way that dancers were selected and rehearsed. My plan was to engage four dance schools and allocate some of the songs to each of them. Every school would select their own performers, choreograph their own routines and rehearse in their own space. The schools would be paid for their contribution including rehearsals and would be responsible for their own chaperones and child protection policy (where applicable). I wanted two narrators situated at a lectern so they could consult the script if necessary, with a good microphone system, and each would understudy the other. I decided not to have projected images during the performance because many people had told me that it distracted them from what was happening on stage at the Nottingham shows.

I booked the Lowther Pavilion Theatre at Lytham St Annes near Blackpool for Sunday 2nd October 2011 with a 'get in' time of 1pm, for a combined technical and dress rehearsal at 2pm with the performance starting at 7pm. Prior to that date I had supplied the theatre with all the necessary sound CDs, running order and given some guidance to sound requirements with fine details to be arranged at the technical rehearsal.

I had arranged four dance groups as planned but suffered a major problem at the end of August when one had to pull out because of illness of the principal. Nicky Figgins, from Blackpool, whose group were already doing their share of the show agreed to take on the role of the missing school. This meant that they had to choreograph, rehearse and find performers for eleven additional songs and they only had four weeks. In the true tradition of show business they pulled out all the stops and achieved it.

Joan and I travelled to a hotel in Lytham four days before the show and on arrival went into the theatre to makes sure everything was going to plan and were assured it was.

However, we were disappointed that there were no flyers of our 'Billy Fury Dance Show' displayed in and around the theatre, on investigation, these were discovered in an unopened box that we ourselves had delivered to the theatre some weeks before.

A more serious problem occurred on performance day, we arrived at the theatre at 12-30 for the 1pm 'get in' and were kept waiting in the foyer for well over half an hour until I demanded to know what was happening.

We were allowed in to be greeted with an apology and the news that, due to a mistake, the 'multi faceted' venue had been let out for a craft fair the previous day and not converted back to theatre use overnight or in the morning. There were tables and chairs all over the place and one man was slowly moving them away. Our offer of help was refused on grounds of 'elf and safety' so we just had to wait helplessly as plans for our rehearsals were shattered. The dance groups arrived and did bits of rehearsal in whatever space they could find and I found some space and rehearsed the narrators who were excellent. The leaders of the dance groups and the dancers repeatedly asked if they could help prepare the theatre but all offers of help were refused. After 4pm it became apparent that the front stage extension had not been set up. This is essential for a dance show and was delayed even more because the area had been used for storage and had to be cleared. The staff then experienced difficulty fitting the extension.

One group leader threatened to leave and take all her dancers with her if the stage was not available at 6pm. I managed to placate her and we finally got use of the stage at ten minute past six. The dance groups 'blocked' many scenes (this is a term they use for just doing bits of the dance and not the whole piece) but only the first half could be rehearsed. At that point a decision was taken not to rehearse the second half at all. I asked the lighting and sound technicians to 'just use their discretion' because the proper technical rehearsal was impossible.

The show started on time, it was brilliant and the audience loved it. The individual dance groups knew what they had to do. The narrators confidently conveyed the story which was clearly audible throughout the auditorium and no one suspected that the technical staff were 'flying on the seat of their pants'. The only people who knew what had happened were relatives of the performers, they had rehearsed in their own schools during the morning and it had been planned that they would have a break after the dress rehearsal in the afternoon and come back for the performance. They had personal stories of exhausted dancers, missed meals and cancelled hair appointments.

I was pleased that my system of using dance schools who rehearsed in their own space with their own choreography and costumes worked well. I shudder to think what would have happened, because of the theatre rehearsal fiasco, if that had not been done.

These were the groups who defied all the odds to put on a magnificent show:

Nicky Figgins Centre Stage Academy, Bispham, Blackpool
Athina Aristidou
April Shillingford
Bethany Potts
Britney Quirk
Brittany Armer
Courtney Burgess
Elle Daley
Ellie-jay Heatley
Emma Wood
Gavin Field
Hannah Peel
Isabelle Foote
Katy Simms
Kelly Jump
Kelly Smith
Lauren Simkin
Lucy Shuttleworth
Marcus Glen
Meagan Todd
Melissa Banks
Melissa Mills
Miss Nicky Figgins (Principal)
Rachel Sadler
Rosie Grindley
Sammy Jump
Stephanie Nickson
Wei Wei Wu
Yazzmin Knapman-Fletcher

Claire Knight Dance School, Wirral

Abi Preston
Cerys McNee
Claire Pearce
Elizabeth Davidson
Ellena White
Hannah Bennet
Hannah Smith-Richards
Harriet Cavanagh
Katy Poyser
Kirsten Oelofse
Lauren Thirsk
Leah Furlong
Lucy Johnson
Lucy Mulcrone
Lucy Smith-Richards
Luke Bennet
Lucy Bramhall
Olivia Grace
Tim Beckett
Vicky Cowell
Vivien Rees
Wendy Garnett

Whittaker Dance and Drama Centre – Blackpool

Chloe Hinds
Danielle Woodhouse
Grace Holliday
Johanna Rutherford
Laura Eastwood
Lauren Bryne-Fraser
Leonie Bradley
Natalie Coleman
Nikita Coulon
Samantha Enright
Tara Crawforth

Narrators Kimberly Edge and Sarah McFadyen had both trained at the Whittaker Drama Centre. The principals and staff of all the groups and the sixty-three performers worked well together ensuring that the continuity and performance was excellent.

The Lowther Pavilion now has now been refitted with a state-of-the-art seating system giving greater flexibility in how the space is used and allowing a quick transition from a flat floor event to a theatre set up. This is good though I believe it has to be managed effectively.

My next show was only six days away at the Palace Theatre, Mansfield and although this was in a conventional theatre and not a 'multi faceted venue' I contacted them and was assured that they were properly prepared.

A contingent of dancers arriving at the theatre

Hannah who sang the solo part of Sweet Jessica. She and her colleagues can be seen on YouTube title *Sweet Jessica, Hannah Bennet, Billy Fury Dance Show*

I was allocated a share of a dressing room at that show. Fame at last

4: BILLY FURY DANCE
– MANSFIELD PALACE THEATRE

I started planning for my Billy Fury Dance Show at the Palace Theatre at Mansfield, Nottinghamshire in September 2010 for a performance on Saturday 8 October 2011.

Two dancers who had performed in the first show at Nottingham Arts Theatre were members of dance schools at Mansfield Woodhouse and Kirkby in Ashfield respectively. The proprietors of those two schools situated within ten miles of Mansfield immediately agreed to take part in the show. The Rollo Academy of Performing Arts situated in Nottingham also agreed to take part. This left me seeking one further group, I approached another dance academy, Joan and I had attended their shows and were impressed with them. We met the principal one Saturday morning and I agreed a deal for her school to take part. This was the fourth dance group sorted so I was very pleased. Imagine my disappointment on the following Monday when I received an email message from the principal. She had noticed the name of one of the other groups that she did not like. She gave me an ultimatum to get rid of the other group or her group would not take part in the show. I decided to keep the other group and this is an illustration of the rivalry between dance groups and the difficulty which I experienced, some get on really well together and others hate each other.

I agreed to pay additional travelling expenses to the fourth group that I selected. They were situated thirty miles away at Loughborough and had to use a coach to get their dancers and back room staff to Mansfield. I allocated twelve songs to each group, supplied CDs and the script and each group got on with choreographing their routines and rehearsing in their own space.

Vince Eager who had regularly performed with Billy Fury was booked to speak a tribute to Billy Fury at the show but found that he had to cancel through no fault of his own so I filmed him speaking the tribute instead. Vince was present at that famous interview where Larry Parnes put Billy straight on stage following an unofficial interview. The YouTube name is *Billy Fury by Vince Eager, Audition at Birkenhead Essoldo*

The 'get in' time was 1pm at the Mansfield Palace Theatre on performance day, Saturday 10 October 2011. Joan and I arrived in good time and the dance groups arrived as planned. An unusual thing happened to Joan as we were preparing for the rehearsal. She was setting up raffle prizes at a table in the auditorium and moving them from the backstage area where we had gone in. Whilst she was in the auditorium the fire curtain was lowered for testing and Joan was stranded in the darkened theatre and not able to get back because of the fire curtain. She shouted for help and fortunately a young lady who was setting up the bar heard her and let her out through the bar area. We often have a laugh about it when we are in a theatre and the safety curtain comes down.

Mansfield Palace Theatre host many dance shows and they are good at it. The back stage facilities are excellent, everyone was gathered together and were given instruction on procedures, health, safety and backstage etiquette. The dress and technical rehearsal went well and the performers had some time off before the show which started at 7pm. The show was a great success, it was enjoyed by performers and audience alike and received enthusiastic applause. Of course there were many family and friends of the performers as well as Billy Fury fans in the audience. I was very proud of everyone involved and include names of the groups and performers who took part:-

Narrators
Georgia Munnion
Helen Greatorex

Excelsior School of Dance and Gymnastics – Mansfield Woodhouse
Alana Mullis
Amelia Pidduck
Angela Stirland
Chloe Carlin
Chloe Smalley
Demi Hodgkinson
Ellie Pheasant
Emily Sykes
Emily Wiseman
Greer Taylor

Hollie Matthews
Jazmine Vessey
Kaye Beastall
Kimberley Smith
Lauren Banks
Lauren Pidduck
Leah Carlin
Lucy Taylor
Natalie Smith
Natasha Vessey
Olivia Weaver
Rachael Spencer
Rebecca Wiseman
Rebecca Spencer
Samuel Holden
Shannan Clay
Sian McIntyre
Tammy Wilcockson
Tia Clay

Christine March School of Dance – Kirkby in Ashfield
Amber Otten-Miller
Amy Marshall
Cora Vanaman
Jessica Johnson
Katie Beecroft
Niamh Beardsley

Charnwood School of Dance, Loughborough
Amie Cunningham
Amy Walker
Angela Mawman
Cathy Barnes
Charlotte Davis
Chloe French
Danielle-Grace Gudger
Ellie Tack
Emily Ralph

Emily Rice
Emma Doherty
Evie Marshall
Evie Martin
Hannah Lanes
Hannah Purvis
Heather Rignall
Helen Pilkington
Holly Oliver
Holly Prangley
Jodie Green
Joella Senior
Georgia James
Katherine Smith
Maisie Wade
Megan Price
Molly Ogle
Molly Sutton
Rebekkah North
Sophie Barraclough
Stacey McGrath
Stacey Pitchford

Rollo Academy of Performing Arts – Nottingham
Abbey Marvin
Amy Meadows
Amber Hudson
Ashleigh Morris
Beth Ursell
Charlotte Burrows
Chloe Hopcroft
Destinee Needham
Erin Keogh
Ffion King
Gabbie Tempest
Ella Roebuck-Swain
Fabiane Leame

Georgia Buda
Lillie Wildman
Lydia Thacker
Melissa Dudley
Millie Dearie
Mollie McGugan
Shanade Williams
Shayna McPherson

The 2 narrators and 87 dancers made a total of 89 cast members and during the finale I made a heartfelt speech which was videoed by a friend and loaded to YouTube with the name *Michael Parkinson's Billy Fury Show, Mansfield Palace* so I have been able to use it to print the actual words that I used 'ladies and gentlemen, if this were a television programme eighty six of these dancers would have been thrown out like so much dross and we would just be left with one who would be considered the champion. To me, we have eighty seven champion dancers tonight and I am grateful to every one of them'. The video finished with the dancers acknowledging applause from the audience.

A couple spoke to me after the show who told me that they live in Manchester and had attended the Billy Fury Dance Show at Lytham St Annes on the previous Sunday. They enjoyed it so much that they travelled to Mansfield six days later to attend this show which of course had a different cast. I wanted to know which show they had enjoyed the most but they insisted that they derived equal amounts of enjoyment from each and were interested in the varied approach to the same songs.

The only slight reservation that I had about this show was that sometimes there were little breaks between some of the numbers so the continuity was not quite as slick as it had been at Lytham St Annes or Nottingham. I made myself a note to do better at my next show at the Floral Pavilion, New Brighton which overlooks the Mersey where young Ronald Wycherley had worked on a tug boat before achieving fame as Billy Fury.

I made a donation of £521 to Jessie's Fund from the shows at Lytham and Mansfield bringing the total to over £5700.

A group of dancers before the start of the show

5: Billy Fury Dance – Floral Pavilion New Brighton

In March 2011 I booked The Floral Pavilion Theatre at New Brighton, Wirral for a performance of my Billy Fury Dance Show on 1 April 2012. It is an attractive venue overlooking the Mersey Estuary with Liverpool Docks on the other side of the water. Booking this attractive 800 plus fixed seated auditorium with plush surroundings and state of the art lighting, sound and acoustics is the most ambitious project I have ever undertaken.

I had already used the Claire Knight Dance School, in my show at Lytham St Annes in October 2011 so they were first on my list. They were soon joined by Wallasey School of Ballet and Anamal Dance Company of Hoylake so all three companies were from the Wirral and happy to work together. I formed an agreement with another dance school who originally wanted to be included but pulled out. I decided to ask Nicky Figgins, although her academy is based near Blackpool and would incur additional travel expense to me. I was full of admiration for them because they had pulled all the stops out to replace the group who had pulled out of the Lytham show only four weeks before the performance date.

This is part of my message to them:

'Hi Nicky, I would like you to take part in my Billy Fury Show at the Floral Pavilion, New Brighton on Sunday 1 April 2012. This opportunity has arisen because a group have pulled out stating the reason that they have just received their competition schedule for 2012 which clashes with my show. I don't understand how a dance group can state categorically that they will take part in a show and then pull out. By a huge coincidence the three scenes are those that you did at Lytham, 4,9 and 13' Best wishes Michael.

This is the reply I received:-

Thank you Michael. When I opened my school 6 years ago after many years of successfully performing I promised myself I would train my pupils but also give them the opportunity to perform in fantastic shows along the way. As far as I am concerned I am not only a teacher to teach but I can give these children memories that will last forever. I believe that live entertainment has been dying for years and am proud to be in a show that brings that back. I will also never let anyone down, if you say yes then mean yes. We are really looking forward to it again although when I told my pupils that we were doing the original 11 they said but what about Glad all over and Hippy Hippy Shake!!!!!!!! they're very funny NickyXX

That was a lovely response to my request and the reference to the two songs has been echoed by many dance groups, they are both fast and dancers love performing to them.

So my revised line up was fixed:-

Claire Knight Dance School *Wirral,* Wallasey School of Ballet *Wallesey Wirral;*

Nicky Figgins Stage School *Blackpool and* Anamal Dance Company *Hoylake Wirral.*

The next objective was to find two narrators. After much work I selected Zoe Vaux and Lois Moon, both from Liverpool. After I had agreed terms with Zoe and Lois I received a further application from Jenny Hammond, an experienced TV presenter so decided to include all three with Zoe playing the role of leader and the other two joint narrators. It transpired that Zoe and Jenny had previously worked together and were looking forward to being involved again. They arranged rehearsals in their own homes and I met them for a final rehearsal at the Queen's Royal Hotel (where Joan and I were staying) on 27 of March. I invited Jean Wycherley (Billy Fury's Mother) to the show but was told that she would be away in Germany so would not be able to attend.

The first scene of my show includes a song called 'Sweet Jessica' it was written by Susan Raasay who was Associate Director of London Studio Centre's 'Oh What a Lovely War'. I had collaborated with them in putting on three performances of that show at the Nottingham Arts Theatre in 2005. Susan learned about Jessie's story during preparation for the shows and was inspired to write the song. It had been performed by the Claire Knight group at Lytham St Annes with singer Hannah Bennet. I wanted to video this for loading to YouTube in a studio setting because videoing in a live performance is difficult with varying lighting conditions and other factors. Joan and I went to Claire Knights Dance Studio which is now known as Irby Dance Studio four days before the performance day where Claire had arranged for some of the dancers to stay after the normal lessons and some to come in specially. The first attempt looked terrible because they were performing in the middle of a huge studio with no backdrop but Claire said 'no problem I can draw a partition across' so they tried again but this time the sound was weak because it was coming from the other side of the partition. Claire said 'we have a speaker this side, I just need to alter the connection to the amplifier' so we tried again but this time I noticed that some of the dancers were masked by the ones in front, I said to the group 'if you can't see the camera, the camera can't see you' Claire changed things taking sight lines into consideration and we tried again. Eventually I was satisfied and thanked the dancers, one of them said they were pleased to do it for Jessie's Fund. Claire, Hannah and the dancers put a lot of effort and stayed late to do this video for me, I felt a bit guilty because I had put them to so much trouble but the next day received a message from Claire thanking me for my efforts and stating 'they had learned a lot from me' that made me feel twelve feet tall, the YouTube title is *Sweet Jessica, Hannah Bennet, Billy Fury Dance Show.* Hannah is now her first year at college in London (February 2018).

Joan and I had travelled to New Brighton on 27 March and I had a meeting with the Floral Pavilion management and technical team. I was able to convey my wishes about sound, lighting and continuity to them. It was also arranged that I would be allocated a technical area to myself because I planned to film the show on my Super VHS camera which housed a full size three hour super VHS tape.

On performance day everything went to plan. The performers arrived in good time, Joan busied herself preparing the raffle and prizes for Jessie's Fund. The dress/tech rehearsal was under way and I was situated on my own in the technical area at the rear of the theatre.

I was approached by a member of staff who told me that Billy Fury's mother was in a car outside the theatre and wanted to know if she could come to the show. I went down to see her and arranged to introduce her to the audience at the end of the show. I had been planning to make a speech but asked Jean to do so instead. I suggested to Jean that she announce an encore of 'Half Way to Paradise'. I went back to my position, the rehearsal finished and everyone had a couple of hours off before showtime.

We returned to the Floral Pavilion in good time to see the audience arriving and just before the show started I returned to my position in the technical area with the Super VHS camera. I needed to continually adjust the camera focus according to lighting conditions and was all prepared to do so. The show started and I was totally unprepared for something that happened to me. Everything was superb, the lighting, sound, costumes, colour, dancing, speech all brilliant. I suddenly dissolved into tears, not just moist eyes but uncontrollable shaking and tears of emotion. Everything that I had been working for since I first had the idea of the show worked. I was a total wreck and all idea of operating the camera vanished. I was not able to compose myself until just before the interval and it was such a relief to meet people and hear how they were enjoying the show.

The second half started and I was not much better and towards the end of the show I made my way to the front row of the auditorium leaving the camera running but unattended. When the finale finished I introduced Billy's Mother to the audience and shared a few words to the audience with 91 year old Jean. When this was finished Jean suggested an encore of 'Halfway to Paradise' but she did not sit down next to me as planned. Instead she grabbed the microphone from me and proceeded to accompany her son singing. The audience loved it and gave her a standing ovation. This can be seen on YouTube with terrible picture quality but the sound indicates what she did, the title is *Jean Wycherley, Mother of Billy Fury, Speaks and sings, Tribute.*

There were 118 dancers and 3 narrators in the show:-

Leader, Zoe Vaux, Narrators, Jenny Hammond & Lois Moon

Anamal Dance Company, Hoylake
Georgina Barlow
Harry Barnes
Jodie Beauchamp
Evie Cheung
Frankie Clarke
Rosie Connor
Annie Corke
Errin Coull
Oliver Courtney
Amy Cowley
Beth Cumming
Sophia Dollery
Alex Doran
Jessica Doran
Sophie Evans
Libby Farrar

Megan Fletcher
George Fletcher
Mya Flowerdew
Rebecca Gerety
Courtney Goddard
Lucy Harrison
Kelly Hayden
Charlie Holmes
Aimee Jackson
Hollie Amy Jarvis
Ella Johansen
Jodie Kelly
Erin Kidd
Adam Ledgerton
Ellie Malone
Belen Manley
Kelsey McCarthy
Margarita McGrath
Leah McNay
Chris McNeilis
Stacie McNeilis
Rebecca Morgans
Katie Moruzzi
Danuelle Murray
Anna Riley
Brogan Roy
Margaret Saunders
Olivia Smith
Grace Speed
Izzi Steele
Jen Suaby
Laura Suckley
Hannah Waywell
Pippa Welch

Claire Knight Dance School, Wirral
Tim Beckett

Hannah Bennet
Luke Bennet
Harriet Cavanagh
Gemma Crutchley
Lizzie Davidson
Leah Furlong
Wendy Garnett
Olivia Grace
Emma Hopwood
Elise Johnson
Lucy Johnson
Cerys McNee
Millie Metz
Lucy Mulcrone
Kirsten Oelofse
Claire Pearce
Katy Poyser
Abi Preston
Viv Rees
Lauran Thirsk
Ellena White

Nicky Figgins Centre Stage Academy, Blackpool
Athina Aristidou
Brittany Armer
Melissa Banks
Mr Gavin Field
Miss Nicky Figgins
Miss Rosie Grindley
Miss Kelly Jump
Samantha Jump
Karis Lomax
Melissa Mills
Stephanie Nickson
Hannah Peel
Britney Quirk
Lauren Simkin

Katy Simms
Miss April Shillingford
Lucy Shuttleworth
Miss Wei Wei Wu
Emma Wood

Wallasey School of Ballet, Liscard
Nicola Barr
Lisa Beattie
Chloe Bryan
Molly Chrishan
Laura Collison
Katie Dodd
Faye Edwards
Natalie Edwards
Melissa Fearnley
Erin Haig
Zoe King
Katie Lewis
Katie Lindon
Sophie Lyons
Sophie McGregor
Sophie Nelson
Sarah Perkins
Rachel Pickford
Melissa Pugh
Bethany Richards
Hannah Ridge
Jessica Roberts
Kimberley Roberts
Rachel Sefton
Katie Sheridan
Kirsty Walsh
Nicole Yee

One of the songs in the show was 'In My Room' Larry Parnes, Billy's manager had wrongly claimed that it was written by Billy Fury but in fact it had been written by fellow Liverpudlian Jimmy Campbell who died on 12 February 2007.

He is commemorated by a seat and plaque situated on the sea front about a mile from the Floral Pavilion. Jimmy's family were regular visitors to the Hotel where Joan and I were staying so I gave them tickets and they attended the show as my guests. Katie Sheridan from the Wallasey School of Ballet performed a solo routine to this lovely song, the YouTube title is *Billy Fury In My Room, Wallasey School of Ballet*

Other videos from the show are on my YouTube channel Michael notthatone Parkinson

I have selected one of each group as suggested viewing:-

Billy Fury That's All Right Floral Pavilion New Brighton
Billy Fury Running Around, Floral Pavilion New Brighton
Billy Fury Maybe Tomorrow, Floral Pavilion New Brighton
Billy Fury Died 1983 Speaks & sings Forget Him

It had been a memorable and emotional experience for me. To see things that I had planned come to fruition, words I had written spoken so well, the combination of Billy Fury singing and the dancing routines culminating in the standing ovation for Jean was brilliant.

As a result of the show I donated £530 to Jessie's Fund.

Myself with Jean Wycherley

6: BILLY FURY DANCE
– FLORAL PAVILION
SHAW THEATRE, LONDON

In 2015 I decided to put my show on in London using professional performers and asked Cora Vanaman if she would be interested in directing it for me. Cora had an impressive CV of song, dance, choreography, teaching and narration and she had performed in my first Billy Fury Dance Show at Nottingham Arts Theatre. Though she was only fourteen at the time she had danced, narrated and choreographed routines for the other dancers. In addition, in October 2011 she took part in my Billy Fury Dance Show at the Palace Theatre Mansfield, as a member of the Christine March Dance School where she had been a member from the age of three. In that show the script required a group of dancers to sing the 23rd psalm (as part of the scene depicting the death and funeral of Billy Fury). Two days before the show most of the girls dropped out of the singing leaving just two who were to sing as a duet. On the day before the show the other girl dropped out and I asked Cora to sing solo which she did beautifully. She had then gone on to the Mountview Academy of Theatre Arts in London where she had done a Foundation Course in Musical Theatre. When I contacted Cora to ask if she was interested in directing my London show she had just finished at Mountview so the timing was ideal.

We held a meeting where we discussed various things and arranged a second meeting for a week later. At that second meeting Cora introduced Craig Canning who she wanted as assistant director to work with her over rehearsals and the shows and we discussed many aspects of the show, content, cast required, rehearsals and much more.

In the meantime I investigated various theatres in and around London before deciding to hire the Shaw Theatre situated near St Pancras Station and the

British Library on Euston Road. The plush 446 seater theatre is only a mile and a half from the West End and appeared ideal. It is part of the Pullman Hotel, owned by the Accor Group. There would be fourteen performances between 14th and 23rd April 2016 with some matinees. The difficult part of promoting a show is that you have to book a theatre long before the event so this was done in June 2015.

The next obstacle was rehearsal space, again necessary long before the show and not easy to find in London but we found what appeared to be ideal premises, Pulse Studios, situated on Liverpool Road Islington and booked the studio for 13 days starting on 29 March with final date on 12th April 2016 before our dress rehearsal at the theatre the day before the first performance. At that point Cora and Craig had not seen the studios. I had gone in, looked around, done the booking and paid a deposit of £768.

Our next objective was to audition performers and I formed an agreement with SCA Management at Italia Conti and an audition took place in their premises near the Barbican on 20 October. I loaded video clips to YouTube under the title *Billy Fury Dance audition, Michael Parkinson,* Many dancers and a narrator took part in the audition and the hard working but relaxed environment can be seen on the video. When the audition finished Cora, Craig and myself were on a high. It was the first really enjoyable episode in the planning for the show. We had a couple of hours to spare before our train back to Nottingham and I suggested that we go to the rehearsal studios so that Cora and Craig could see the facilities. I telephoned Pulse Studio to tell them that we were calling in but no one answered even though they should have been open. We decided to go anyway and on arrival found the studio dark and locked with a notice on the door – 'Studio closed until further notice. All lessons and bookings cancelled' Our feelings of elation were dashed and though rehearsals were not due to start for five months, I was worried about the outcome, what was going to happen and what about the deposit I had paid?

On the train back to Nottingham Cora busied herself with her copious notes about the audition and selection ideas. We had already decided on a second audition to look at performers who had applied to us individually and were planning to hold that at Pulse Studios.

I telephoned my contact at the studio the next morning and learned that there was a huge dispute between the owner of the dance studio Jonathon Laidlaw and the owner of the building. This had resulted in the studio being closed. I was given the telephone number of the studio owner and had to leave a message so I feared he would not contact me. To my surprise Johnathon phoned me a couple of hours later and explained the situation to me. It was not good and there was little chance of it being resolved. He advised me that it would be better to cancel the rehearsal bookings and he would reimburse the £768 deposit that I had paid. He promised that the money would be paid back by bank transfer and to my delight he telephoned me within twenty minutes to say it was done. Imagine my relief when I checked my bank statement to see the money had been repaid. I spoke to Johnathon whilst preparing this book and he told me that the dispute with the owner of the building had led to the closure of his dance studio business.

My next task was to find another rehearsal space and discovered Husky Studios at Amelia Street which is situated underneath the railway arches at Elephant and Castle. It was closer to central London so more expensive than Pulse but I booked various dates for our rehearsals and 10 November for our second audition. Cora, Craig and I attended this audition.

Cora believes that dancers should warm up before dancing because it helps to avoid stress and strains. She put the dancers through a vigorous warm up and it can be seen on YouTube title *Dance Warm Up, Leader Cora Vanaman, Husky*. If you think that dancing is easy, take a look at this. An audition video can also be seen on YouTube title *Billy Fury Dance audition 2 Husky*. Cora made her final selection of dancers and we agreed on the narrator so these were the performers selected to take part in the 14 Billy Fury Dance Shows at the Shaw Theatre:-

		From:
Ronald Wycherley	Ryan Mockridge	Hastings, Sussex
Billy Fury	Charles Ames	London Borough of Wanstead
Narrator (Mickey)	Scott Westwood	West Bromwich, W. Midlands
Dancers	Becky Basset	Liverpool, Merseyside
	Paige Blackwell	Borehamwood, Herts.
	Ellen Bleasdale	Warrington, Cheshire
	Eleanor Byrne	Dublin, Southern Ireland
	Abigail Cleary	Dundee, Scotland
	Hollie Dorman	Underwood, Nottinghamshire
	Lara Greenhow	Coventry, Warwickshire
	Alice Gribben	Scunthorpe, Lincolnshire
	Zoe Price	Hullbridge, Essex

I got contracts agreed by all the performers and loaded informative videos to YouTube of Cora and Craig speaking about their involvement in the show. The video titles are:-

Billy Fury Dance Show, Cora Vanaman, Director
Billy Fury Dance Show, Craig Canning hit by David Essex

In the second video Craig talks to Cora about being hit in the face whilst performing as a stuntman with David Essex.

Cora located accommodation for herself and Craig which I viewed and booked for the duration of rehearsals and shows, she took measurements of the performers and arranged for a dressmaker to make some of the special costumes and others were bought on Ebay.

On 7 February 2016 Cora sent me this message:

'Hi Michael, Hope you are OK. I have just spent the entire day with my Dad and we have completely reworked the script for the narrator. Whilst the content of your script was very factual and informative, I hope you understand that to work in this type of show would have been extremely difficult, therefore the script needed to be more audience friendly and entertaining. The revised script, albeit a first draft at this stage, has been tailored to suit Scott and will allow him to use his skills to interact with both the cast and the audience and I have every confidence that it will work well. I appreciate that it only summarises key points out of your original script but for a dance show I felt it important to keep the focus on entertainment. Please find it enclosed for your perusal'. Thanks Cora

This was a bombshell because I liked my original script and there had never been any problems with it in previous shows. However, I took the view that it would be pointless to pay a young person to direct my show, because I wanted a young feel to it and then stifle her initiative. Apart from that I liked some of the ideas that Cora and her father had introduced. Whilst researching this book I discovered that Cora's grandfather was in fact an American GI who had been sent to England in 1944 prior to the D-Day Normandy landings. He had met and eventually married a young lady from Mansfield, Nottingham. They lived in America for a few years before moving to England. The result of this was that Cora'a Father needed no introduction to American music and his knowledge was invaluable when he assisted his daughter Cora in revising my script. A few years later young Ronald Wycherley was influenced by records brought in by American workers that he met whilst working on a tug boat in Liverpool docks. It is strange how the Billy Fury story and my London show had such a strong American influence.

I am grateful to Universal Music, London and Lisa Voice who gave permission for the Billy Fury tracks to be used in all my Billy Fury shows. The dress and technical rehearsals went on with the normal amount of hassle and the first performance on Thursday 14 April was well received by the audience. I sat on the front row with my camera mounted on a tripod and videoed some performances so that I could edit and load videos to my YouTube channel name Michael notthatone Parkinson.

The first scene starts with Heartbeat playing, Ronald Wycherley enters stage, dances a little, goes to sit downstage right, starts writing. Mickey enters, music fades but remains on quietly, Mickey speaks '*The dockside, Liverpool. What a place. It's grey, it's dark, but d'you know what, I love it, Oh, I'm Mickey by the way, yer' alright, I work on the tugs with me mate over there* (indicates 'Ron') '*whatcha whack*' (Ron screws up paper and throws it away, Mickey picks it up and reads paper. *That's my mate Ron. Ronny. And this* (waves paper) *is gonna make him famous one day, you mark my words, cus' my bessie Ronny, he writes dead good songs. Now do you see that, over there,* (points) *that's the Mauretania it's just docked. up. That has come from from the big apple, NYC, the Empire state. It's New York, New York, what a wonderful town. Now something very special is happening in the states at the moment, it's called Rock and Roll. It's gonna' blow your socks off Daddy-o* (in corny American accent, with Elvis move)

(Girl runs through auditorium with record in hand). Girl *Ronny, Ronny, look what I have got for you straight off the boat can you believe it, look here for you.* (Runs on stage) t*his record, Girls, check it out. come on, come on, check it out* Eight girls run on stage, one with a record player (Mickey) *You see because this boat's full of Yanks and these guys bring records, now I'm not talking about How Much is That Doggie in the Window, no, no no, I'm talking about You Ain't Nothing but a Hound Dog, crying all the time, Well you aint' gonna Rabbit, you aint' no friend of mine. (*Girls slap thighs and laugh-Once upon a dream plays, Mickey and four girls exit with record player. Remaining girls dance, joined by Ronnie who is attracted by one of the dancers and the scene ends with the two of them together.

I have included the dialogue from scene one because it illustrates how Ronald Wycherley was influenced by records brought in by American boat workers.

The YouTube video titles in order of performance are:-
Billy Fury Dance 1 Heartbeat, Narration, Once upon a Dream
Billy Fury Dance 2 You're having the last dance with me
Billy Fury Dance 3 Give me your word, Narration

53

Billy Fury Dance 4 It's only make believe
Billy Fury Dance 5 Margo
Billy Fury Dance 6 Running around
Billy Fury Dance 7 I'll never fall in love again
Billy Fury Dance 8 Gonna type a letter
Billy Fury Dance 9 When will you say I love you
Billy Fury Dance 10   Wondrous place
Billy Fury Dance 11   Maybe tomorrow
Billy Fury Dance 12   In thoughts of you
Billy Fury Dance 13   Don't knock upon my door (subject to video blocking)
Billy Fury Dance 14   Nothin' shakin' like the leaves on the trees
Billy Fury Dance 15   I'd never find another you
Billy Fury Dance 16   Like I've never been gone
Billy Fury Dance 17   Run to my loving arms, Dialogue
Billy Fury Dance 18   Colette
Billy Fury Dance 19   That's alright
(last one before the interval so have a cup of tea)
Billy Fury Dance 20   Glad all over
Billy Fury Dance 21   Jealousy
Billy Fury Dance 22   My Christmas Prayer, Narration
Billy Fury Dance 23   Devil or Angel
Billy Fury Dance 24   Somebody else's girl
Billy Fury Dance 25   Hippy Hippy Shake
Billy Fury Dance 26   Because of love
Billy Fury Dance 27   Lady
Billy Fury Dance 28   Last night was made for love
Billy Fury Dance 29 In my room, Narration
Billy Fury Dance 30   In Summer
Billy Fury Dance 31   Psalm 23 Crimond, Sung by dancers
Billy Fury Dance 32   Billy speaks self written words, Forget him
Billy Fury I will, Michael Parkinson Show
Billy Fury Dance 34   I'll never quite get over you, I'm lost without you
Billy Fury Dance 35   A thousand stars, Narration
Billy Fury Dance 36   Halfway to Paradise (Finale)

I have incorporated these song titles as YouTube names but any of them can be blocked either Worldwide or in Certain Countries and that can happen at any time so please understand if you are not able to see certain scenes. Also the type of device you are using can influence what can be seen. At the time of writing (Feb 2018) Billy Fury Dance 13 is subject to blocking by copyright holders.

The artistic and performance side of the show was brilliant and we received many glowing comments from people in the audience, I watched every one of the shows and thoroughly enjoyed them. Readers can form their opinion by looking at some of the YouTube links but the message that shines through to me is that the Billy Fury recordings were as popular with dancers and audiences either amateur or professional as the music of today.

The dancers in full flow

In pensive mood

Joan with Daniel Heeney, a keen Billy Fury fan (See Chapter16)

Joan and I with some of the cast after the final show

Fun at an audition

7: MICHAEL PARKINSON – BILLY FURY BIOGRAPHY

Whilst writing the script and producing my Billy Fury Dance Shows I have put together biographical details and stories about Billy some of which were spoken by cast members or narrators. This forms the base for my short biography of Billy Fury and is not intended to be a full and complete biography.

Billy Fury was a stage name. He was born on 17 April 1940 his real name was Ronald Wycherley. His mother was Sarah Jane Wycherley but for some reason became known as Jean which was the name that she was referred to in my knowledge of her from the year 2009. His father, Albert was in the Army during the 1940s and on returning to civilian life worked as a cobbler. His mother sang a lot and during my conversations with her convinced me that is where young Ron developed his interest in singing and song writing. The family lived in the Dingle area of Liverpool. A young brother, Albert, the same as his father was born on 26 June 1943. Ron attended St Silas Infants School and then went on to Wellington road secondary school. He lost much time at school because of ill health. At six years of age he suffered rheumatic fever and was in Alder Hey Children's Hospital for two months. At the age of 12 he was in hospital again, reportedly this time in Wales. He was not a good patient and after two weeks he got out of the second floor window and climbed down a drainpipe to what he thought was going to be freedom. He was caught in nearby fields and put back in the room with the window securely locked this time.

Ron was given piano lessons from the age of 11 and his parents bought him a guitar for his 14th birthday. He became a good strummer but never progressed beyond three chords. He left school at the age of 15 and worked in an engineering factory for a year. He then worked on a tugboat called 'Formby' in Liverpool docks. Country and western records brought in from America inspired Ron. He formed the Formby Sniffle Gloup (he must have had a sense of humour) and performed in pubs and clubs. Ron liked the lyrics of Hank Williams but decided he wanted to write songs in his own style. This was the deep broken hearted mood evident in much of his work. Ron changed boats but later went to work in a department store. Here he was influenced by a fellow employee, Margo King. He became very fond of her but to Margo Ronnie was just a good friend. He wrote Margo (Don't Go) for her. She got married and emigrated to Australia and did not hear the song for many years.

Ron started to perform gigs and the small audiences were impressed with his singing and song writing abilities. In April 1958 he recorded six demo tracks on a 78 rpm acetate record at Percy Phillips recording studio at 38 Kensington, Liverpool (this premises now has a Blue Plaque). Some reports say that his mother sent this to Larry Parnes but others say that Ron sent a picture of himself and a tape of his songs to impresario Larry Parnes but did not get a reply. He entered a local talent show 'Carroll Levis Discoveries' at the Liverpool Empire but failed to win the heat. His mother wrote again to Larry Parnes who this time replied. Larry invited Ron to see him at the Birkenhead Essoldo on the 1 October 1958. One of his shows, 'The Larry Parnes Extravaganza' was being staged that night. A member of the tour company, who spotted Ron at the Essoldo was Brian Bennett, the backing drummer in Marty Wilde's band. He said later 'Ron had a guitar in a pillow case and wore a pair of brothel creepers, sort of big suede shoes. He had this wonderful swept back blonde hair'. Ron took his guitar out of the bag and sang some of his own songs to Marty Wilde and Larry Parnes. He hoped that Marty would like what he heard and record some of them.

Instead, in an episode that has become music legend, Parnes took Ron on stage during the interval. When the curtains opened a frightened 18 year old made his public debut as a singer. He sang Margo, Maybe Tomorrow and Don't knock upon my door. Ron said later that his knees were literally knocking together but the fans thought it was part of the act. The audience loved his performance and the girls loved his appearance.

At the end of the show Larry Parnes asked Ron to join his Extravaganza tour. He wanted him to appear the very next night when the show moved to the Stretford Essoldo. His parents could not believe it when he got home and told them what had happened. Next morning Ron was packing his suitcase to go to Manchester. His mother got really worried about him going off on his own. Ron convinced her that it was the best chance he would ever have.

Larry Parnes had decided that Ronald Wycherley was no name for a rock star. He told Ron that his first name would be Billy after Billy Cotton the popular bandleader. The second name would be Fury to compensate for his shyness. Ron argued, he wanted to be called Stean Wade, Parnes insisted and the name Billy Fury was born. Billy continued to perform in the Extravaganza shows of Larry Parnes. It was not only his singing voice that impressed the fans. The girls went wild with delight. They screamed louder and louder as he gyrated in a sensual manner. His good looks, singing voice and brilliant stage presentation made him a hit where ever he performed. Billy's influence at this time was Elvis Presley. He copied and accentuated Elvis's sensual moves on stage. In fact he was banned in Dublin because his act was considered to risqué. The show toured extensively and ended in London. Before the end of the tour Billy had more than proved his worth. He got a new, and better, contract, with Larry Parnes. In November 1958 he recorded his first single. This went straight into the top twenty chart in February 59. It was Maybe Tomorrow, written by Billy himself. It was the first song he sang at the Larry Parnes audition. Decca records gave him a seven year recording contract. More singles were released.

A long playing 33rpm record, The Sound of Fury was released in 1960. This reached the top 20 long player chart and has been re-issued in various forms on four occasions. Experts regard it as Britain's finest example of rock n roll, rocka-billy, music. Billy had written all ten songs himself, something unheard of until the Beatles came along. Some were credited to Wilbur Wilberforce, a name Billy used to avoid Larry Parnes taking commission on his writing.

In 1960 Billy had three more hits including Collette. She was, according to Billy, an actress in a subtitled French Film that Billy went to see. He wrote the song on a cigarette packet found on the floor of the cinema. I read his explanation of his song writing method. I find it absolutely amazing. He said 'I get an idea, usually when I'm depressed over some girl. I scribble a lyric and sing the thing straight into a tape recorder. It never gets on to paper until someone at the music publisher puts it there. Then they send me back an arrangement, which I can't read. So, I just record it the way I thought of it'.

His mum, Jean, used to find bits of song on scraps of paper all over the house. This included her bills and important papers.

In the 1960s Billy had more top twenty UK hits than anyone except, The Beatles, Cliff Richard and Elvis Presley. He and his fans were disappointed that he never reached number one. In May 1961 Billy recorded a cover version of Tony Orlando's Halfway to Paradise. This was an immediate hit and got to number three in the charts followed by Jealousy in September 1961, this got to number 2 giving him his highest ever UK singles chart placing.

Billy's heart problem continued to plague him. On some tour dates he had to cut his act short. Sometimes he had to be replaced altogether. The fans were told that he was suffering from exhaustion or the flu.

In 1962 Billy and Larry Parnes flew to Los Angeles to present Elvis Presley with Gold and Silver discs for Decca UK sales. They spent the day on the film set of 'Girls, Girls, Girls'. Billy recalled 20 years later 'We didn't really say much at all, I was on the set watching him, all we got to say to each other was **Hi.** He was one of the nicest people I have ever met, he called everyone Sir'. As a result of this visit Billy's last release of 1962 was 'Because of Love' a song used in the Presley film. Elvis said in a later interview, 'I could not understand Billy Fury, he came all the way from England to see me and all he said was **Hi**'. This was an example of Billy's shyness offstage. Billy's good looks made him a natural for television. His first appearance was in Ted Willis's drama 'Strictly for Sparrows'. He appeared on television in Jack Good's 'Oh Boy' in February 1959. He and Marty Wilde were two favourite performers in another Jack Good television show. This was called 'Boy Meets Girls' and ran for seven months from September 1959. In 1962 he made his film debut in Michael Winner's 'Play it Cool'. He played his own character as Billy Fury in 'I've Gotta Horse', (this is my favourite Billy Fury film). He loved animals and persuaded the studio to include some of his own in 'I've Gotta Horse'. He made a cameo appearance in 'That'll be the Day' and this reached number one in the album charts.

In 1964 he bought a racehorse called 'Anselmo' my wife, Joan, wanted to back the horse in the 1964 Epsom Derby but was too young to place the bet. She persuaded her Mother to do it for her and Anselmo came third at 100 to 1.

I experienced difficulty relating dates and events in Billy's career and found the reason. Larry Parnes knocked a year off Billy's age to make him more attractive to girl fans. On his 22nd birthday he had to pretend to be 21 and so on. This probably made little difference to the fans but it made my research difficult. Frequent health problems started to depress Billy. He struggled through many variety shows and pantomime. 'In Thoughts of You' was his last top ten hit in 1965. Then he began taking time to indulge his love of wildlife. He was always a passionate animal lover, rather surprising, because at the age of two he was badly bitten by a dog. He was permanently scarred on the right cheek and this shows in some of his pictures. Billy signed with the Parlophone label in December 1966. Over the next four years he released eleven singles. He continued to write songs and make TV and radio appearances but his worsening heart condition prevented much promotional work. He played cabaret when health allowed and found peace, whenever possible, at his home in Ockley, Surrey, where he had a mock Tudor mansion with ten acres of land.

I found an interesting story that may have happened around that time, Mark Kozlowski wrote:

My friend Mike Manges, who lives in Akron, Ohio USA is a Billy Fury fan despite being American, he loves 1950s Rock n Roll and he met numerous brits who share similar interests. They introduced him to Billy Fury's work and he loves it so in 2005 there is someone in Ohio playing and loving Billy's recordings. Apparently a friend of his knew someone who, as a child lived in Surrey near where Billy Fury lived at the time. One day, this lad and his friends were sailing their toy boats on a pond, when along came Billy Fury, he stopped and chatted with the boys, asking them what they were doing. He looked at their boats, and said 'I've got a boat'. He went back to his house, and returned with a model yacht, he put it in the pond and sailed it with the boys as if he did that sort of thing every day. Then he looked at his watch and said he had to go. 'What about your boat?' said one of the lads. 'Don't worry' said Billy 'you keep it'. The lad who kept it was a friend of my workmate. My workmate said 'the friend became a real Billy Fury nut after that episode, because Billy was such a nice, down-to-earth guy.

He assembled a large menagerie and played host to the greats of the show business world. Billy eventually needed open heart surgery in December 1971. He could not afford private treatment and was admitted to a National Health Service ward. He started performing again in March 1972 and enjoyed renewed health for a while. By the early 1970s Billy was living in Wales, on a hundred acre farm, with his long term Partner Lisa Rosen. He experienced happiness, breeding horses and sheep. He spent a lot of time bird watching, a boyhood hobby he never gave up. Once he accidentally killed a bird whilst driving, it upset him so much that he brooded for hours. This was the gentle side of Billy, he detested blood sports and attempted to save injured birds. He was involved in work to preserve the Red Kite. He appeared at the 1972 Wembley Rock 'n' Roll Festival. In 73 he appeared in the film 'That'll be the Day'. He did a major tour in 74 and the Russell Harty Show in 76. He needed a second heart operation in 1976 and retired the next year. In 1978 he was declared bankrupt, he owed the Inland Revenue sixteen thousand seven hundred and eighty pounds. Billy always blamed his manager for the problem. In the early days, Larry Parnes paid him a wage but did not take care of the tax. As part of the arrangement with creditors, he re-recorded some hits for K-Tel. He was discharged from bankruptcy the following year and went back into retirement.

In 1982 Billy decided to make a comeback. He went into the studio to record tracks for another album. This was eventually called 'The One and Only' but was not released until after his death. In 1982 he recorded 'Devil or Angel' on the Polydor label.

On the 7th of March 1982 Billy collapsed at the farm in Wales. He suffered partial paralysis and temporary blindness. Lisa drove him to hospital in London and he made a good recovery. Billy performed at a number of venues from June to December 1982. He did many radio interviews. He made three TV appearances; two had to be shown posthumously.

On the 28th of January 1983 Billy, or to be precise, Ronald Wycherley was found unconscious. He was taken from his London apartment and pronounced dead on arrival at St Mary's Hospital, Paddington. The heart weakness that had dogged him all his life had finally claimed him. He was 42 years old. The funeral service was at St John's Wood Church, London on 4 February 1983.

Ironically both Billy Fury and Elvis Presley died at the same age of 42.

He left a legacy of over 340 recordings. He was in the singles charts for 281 weeks and the album charts for 51 weeks. He had a career total of 29 hit singles and 11 top ten hits. His recordings are regularly played on Radio and his films are being sold and watched today.

A DVD video 'His Wondrous Story' was released in 2007 by Odeon Entertainment Ltd, it has achieved excellent sales and is still available for purchase today.

A DVD video 'The Sound of Fury' was released in April 2015 and has reached number one in the UK Music DVD charts, it is available for home viewing and has been shown in many cinemas and extensively on BBC television.

The final episode in the story of Ronald Wycherley was the death of his Mother, Jean on the 17 May 2017 aged 96. Joan and I travelled to Liverpool for the funeral which went from her house in Aigburth called 'Wondrous Place.' The service was at St Anne's Church, Aigburth where Colin Paul spoke a tribute to Jean and then sang 'In Thoughts of You' in a voice trembling with emotion. I have put video clips together from that day and happier times backed by Billy Fury singing 'In Thoughts of You' in my tribute to her and loaded this to YouTube, at the time of writing (Feb 2018) this has attracted nearly four thousand views and lovely comments, I believe this is a token of the admiration and respect that people had for Jean and her influence on the career of her son. The YouTube name is

Billy Fury Mother died age 96 Tribute, In Thoughts of You

Numerous videos of Billy Fury including interviews and songs are available on YouTube enabling people of today and future generations, in many countries, to discover the songs and backing tracks that dedicated followers have been enjoying for many years. In my opinion the words of the songs are as relevant today as when he first recorded them.

A Blue Plaque marks the London residence at St John's wood.

Thank you Lee Fry for use of his copyright Billy Fury picture.

8: Billy Fury Graveside Tribute

by Michael Parkinson

Tuesday 28 January 2014 was the 31st anniversary of the death of Billy Fury, I usually go to London each Wednesday so had decided to go to the grave at Mill Hill Cemetery in North London on that day to video the floral tributes that had been placed the previous day. I woke at around 3am on the Wednesday with an idea that I should speak a tribute to Billy at the grave. I tried to dispel the thought from my mind and get back to sleep but could not, the idea would not go away. I decided that a certain scene of my show script would be ideal so, went down stairs, switched the computer on and printed off the appropriate page. I placed the A4 page into a thin plastic folder and placed it by the front door with my small tripod to take with me. I went back to bed and on wakening a few hours later I was disappointed to see that it was raining heavily. Joan told me that she had heard the forecast and it was going to rain for most of the day in London but I said 'I will still go to the grave, perhaps it will have stopped by the time I get there'.

When the train reached St Pancras it was 'chucking it down' but I decided to go anyway. I travelled on the underground Northern line but on arrival at Edgware it was still raining. I went on a 221 bus and it was still raining as I got off at Salcombe Gardens. As I walked up Milespit Hill I questioned my sanity. It was cold, raining heavily and blowing a gale but I thought 'it may get a little better when I get to the grave'. It didn't and as I walked along I realised that I was the only living person in the cemetery (apart from the ground staff who were sheltering in their shed). I tried videoing whilst standing with the iPhone under my chin out of the rain but speaking, holding the phone and script was impossible. I gave up on that method and placed my camera on my portable tripod halfway along the grave and knelt on the stone surround at the foot of the grave. I leaned forward so that I could hold the script and plastic cover over the phone to keep it dry and had to lean forward to read it. My first two attempts of reciting the words were terrible, I tried again but was still not satisfied. I was trembling with cold and saturated so had to stop. I went down to the Chapel, squeezed water from my trouser legs and played my video. It was not good, the rain on the plastic cover and the wind sounded terrible and I had stuttered a bit on the third take as well. I decided that it was not good enough for YouTube but looked again at home the next day and loaded it with 'apologies for the background noise caused by rain on the camera cover'. Within three hours the video had received many views and a comment from 'soundsmagic' saying 'that was fantastic - the rain makes it sound like the crackles on an old record, the words you spoke were great and thank you' that comment meant a lot to me and illustrates the beauty of YouTube that a complete stranger wrote such words of encouragement. The video can be seen on YouTube under the title *Billy Fury Graveside Tribute by Michael Parkinson* at the time of writing (Feb 2018) it has had over forty four thousand views, 268 likes only 3 dislikes and 60 comments, it is receiving about 40 views every day. I believe it shows how many people are still interested in Billy Fury.

These are the words that I recited on the video:-

'29th of January 2014, yesterday was the 31st anniversary of the death of Ronald Wycherley, Billy Fury. Billy left a legacy of over 340 recordings. He was in the singles charts for 281 weeks and the album charts for 51 weeks. He had a career total of 29 hit singles and 11 top ten hits. His recordings are regularly played on Radio and his films are being watched and sold today. He is buried here at Paddington Cemetery, Mill Hill, North London. The grave is frequently visited and maintained by fans. The headstone bears the inscription, *His Music Gave Pleasure to Millions*. His music still gives pleasure to millions. Here we are 31 years later, listening to his unique voice and those lovely songs, many written by Billy himself. A bronze statue stands on the riverside at Liverpool. It features Billy looking out over the Mersey where he used to work on a tugboat. It took The Sound of Fury Fan Club six years four months to raise over forty thousand pounds for the statue. The inscription on the plaque reads:-

BILLY FURY (RONALD WYCHERLEY)
17th APRIL 1940 TO 28 JANUARY 1983
LEGENDARY BRITISH ROCK 'N' ROLL STAR
MAJOR UK CHART ARTIST
OUTSTANDING AND CHARISMATIC LIVE PERFORMER,
SONGWRITER, ANIMAL LOVER AND GENTLE MAN
THIS STATUE HAS BEEN ACHIEVED THROUGH THE
DEDICATION OF BILLY FURY FANS WORLDWIDE
SCULPTED BY FELLOW LIVERPUDLIAN TOM MURPHY

These words are a lasting memorial to Billy Fury. People often ask why Billy Fury was buried in London and not his native Liverpool. Of course he had been away from Liverpool for over twenty years. I was told by a fan who lives nearby that Billy had lived close to Mill Hill for a while so he chose Mill Hill as his final resting place. His grave is situated at one of the highest points of the cemetery, next to the roadway where a bench seat memorial to Billy is situated.

The Sound of Fury Fan Club is heavily involved with the management and maintenance of the grave and the bench seat. Regrettably the original dove on the top was damaged, perhaps deliberately, but possibly accidentally by a grass strimmer but an attempt to remove one of the photos was deliberate and resulted in damage. Both of the original photos, one loosened and both faded, were therefore replaced in consultation and with the help of Frank Bull a dedicated fan and friend of Mrs Jean Wycherley and Billy's manager, Hal Carter. Frank Bull, then hailing from Enfield where he was an undertaker with obvious connections in the trade arranged for the original photos that were made in Italy and paid for by fans, to be produced and fitted. Frank, together with Hal Carter, Billy's mum Jean and several fans attending Mill Hill, some of whom later became the SOF team, had previously had a surround put in place in addition to the oval photos. All of this was graciously permitted by Billy's long-term companion Ms Lisa Voice, who owns the grave. The fan club also pays to have the grave cleaned professionally once a year and has the non-formal but very generous assistance of a dedicated reasonably local fan, Marina Weedon, for general tidying and checking up on the sites condition. I met Marina on my first visit to the grave and subsequently at my Shaw Theatre Show, her story is included in chapter twenty.

Many fans put floral and written tributes on the grave throughout the year and the way it looks is a testimony to his continued popularity.

The headstone on the grave

9: Angela Colette Peacock

I understand you are doing some research on Billy and how he has impacted on his fan's lives, and thought I would write to tell you about my wonderful dad, and how Billy was a huge part of his life, and ours.

My dad is Frank Bull, he sadly passed away from pancreatic cancer in April 2019. He is very well known amongst the Billy Fury fan club circles and was a huge Billy fan. Dad knew Billy's brother Albie and his mum Jean. Jean came to dad's wedding to his lovely second wife Margaret (known as 'Mig'), in 1993. Margaret sadly passed away in 2011. Dad and Mig's first dance at their wedding was 'I Love How You Love Me'.

Dad was a lifelong Billy fan and was a huge driving force behind the statue in Liverpool. He bought his first 45 single aged 15 and that was the start. Dad saw Billy live numerous times, had two copies of all his singles, albums and CDs (just in case!).

Dad told me that he saw Billy just after I was born and told him he had just become a father. He said the next time he saw Billy he asked 'How's Angela?'. Dad was over the moon that Billy had remembered the name of his baby daughter, my name! I guess it was things like that that endeared Billy to his fans and explains why he is still so loved by them. Dad took me to see him when he made his comeback, a wonderful memory.

My brother and I recall Billy's music being played from before we can remember, in fact, where most parents sang 'Rock-a-bye Baby' and nursery rhymes to their kids, dad sang 'Halfway to Paradise' and other Billy songs to us! I can't ever remember a time when Billy wasn't in our lives somewhere.

One of dads most treasured possessions was an engraved tie pin which had belonged to Billy, this was given to dad by Jean. It has 'Play It Cool' engraved on it. Dad left it to me and I also treasure it. Dads favourite Billy song was 'I'd Never Find Another You', closely followed by 'Halfway to Paradise'. I remember when we were young, my dad and brother singing along, into a broom handle, as a duet, to Colette (my middle name!).

It was only fitting that as much as Billy was a huge part of dads life, he was also a huge part of his funeral service. We played Billy as dad came into the church and as he left and at the graveside. I chose the song 'I Will' as its my favourite Billy song, my brother chose 'Wondrous Place'.

My brother plays Billy songs all the time as it helps him feel close to dad. I struggle sometimes as it still hurts so much that he is gone, but one thing is for certain – I bet dad and Billy have had a right old chat wherever they are now!

I hope this helps with what you are doing. It has been very therapeutic for me to write this and remember my lovely dad and the very talented Billy Fury who was such a big part of our lives.

Dad with dark hair and glasses next to Billy Fury

Dad on his 74th birthday

Billy Fury, picture supplied by Lee Fry

10: ANN WALKER

Like thousands of other girls, I fell in love with the voice of Billy Fury when I first heard 'Halfway to Paradise' on the radio. Then when I saw his photograph in my 'pop' magazines, I was completely hooked. I've lived in Yorkshire almost all my life and shortly after I 'discovered' Billy I saw in the local paper that he was coming to Wakefield (about 12 miles away), I think the theatre was called the Playhouse. So I immediately booked tickets – I think everybody fell totally in love with this blonde, blue-eyed, gorgeous young man with the most amazing voice. That night, I decided that somehow I had to meet him in the future. There was no question about waiting outside the stage door, we had two buses to catch to get us back home.

It was the following summer I saw that he was going to appear at The Windmill, Great Yarmouth. I think I was about 17, it was very early 60's. I booked tickets immediately – front row – and got my thinking cap on. That's when I decided to try and paint another portrait of him (I had already done one but it wasn't very good). I completed it, was quite pleased with it, so I then wrote to the theatre manager asking if I could meet Billy to give it to him. I assured him I wasn't a hysterical teenager (I gave myself a good reference!). Imagine my excitement when I received a letter back saying I could, and to take that letter with me.

I was speechless when I met Billy, but he was so lovely. He seemed very shy, as I was, but he loved the painting (said he did anyway!). I honestly can't remember much about the conversation, but the 'double exposure' photo of the two of us was taken that night. Although it's 'two photos on one' (the person who took it forgot to roll the camera film on), I love it. Anyway something strange happened – some people came in (about three, all male, no idea who they were I was too preoccupied with seeing Billy) and they were carrying Karl Denver's clothes that he'd had on in the car accident the previous night. They must have been to visit him in hospital. I think it was reported that he wasn't badly injured but I recall seeing blood on the clothing. I felt it was a deeply personal time for them all, so I picked up my handbag and indicated I was leaving. Billy had this way of eye contact, he smiled, thanked me again and I left.

I know that on one occasion when I left, Billy walked with me to the stage door leading out into the street. We could hear that there were lots of girls waiting outside – Billy gave me a peck on the cheek and retreated. As I left I heard one girl say 'Who is she'? I remember thinking I'm just a fan, like you, but a very lucky one. I said nothing and let them wonder! I thought it was at the Windmill, but it can't have been because that was the Karl Denver episode when I left on my own.

I've lost track of years and exact details, but the second time I met him was backstage at the Britannia Pier Theatre, Great Yarmouth. I'd written to the theatre manager, explained a bit of background, and almost by return post (no emails in those days!) I was once again told I could see Billy backstage. He remembered me, had that gorgeous smile on, and said he remembered I lived 'up North'. To think, he'd remembered that, it made me feel so special. I think this must have been the summer of 1964 because I told him I would be 21 the coming August, I was very brave and asked him if he would send me a card! He said he'd do that so I left him my address! The excitement was unbelievable it really was. On that occasion I'd done some pen and ink drawings of him, he loved them. I didn't stay long – as much as I'd have loved to. I've never been a 'pushy' type of person, I would have hated to be seen as a pest, plus the fact I was still so nervous at meeting him. However, Billy came across as being a bit nervous too. He'd just come off stage, he still had his greasepaint on (as you can see from the photo) and I think he was still hyped up from that.

I met Billy again at the Britannia Pier and the last time at the Aquarium Theatre. I didn't do another painting to get backstage at the Britannia this time but I wrote beforehand and was given permission, Billy made me feel so welcome – I was even given a beaker of Coca Cola that I sat and drank with him. I've never spent more than 15 or 20 minutes in his company but this time we chatted easily. His love of animals cropped up and time flew by once we started on that subject, they are my passion too. There were always people buzzing around . On one occasion I remember Marty Wilde was there and I heard him say he'd forgotten where he had parked his car.

I feel quite ashamed to write that I never really bothered to find out much about Larry Parnes or any of Billy's entourage, I just loved the man as Ron or Billy, thats all, and of course, I bought all his records. We spoke as friends especially when I used to tell him about Tammy, my sister's dog, that I walked for her.

Ann had this picture cropped because she was not happy about her hairstyle, what a shame.

Two paintings that Ann did of Billy

A nice picture of Ann, I like the hairstyle

The greeting that Billy wrote on Ann's card August 1964

11: AVRIL DALTON

I was born and brought up in Nelson, Lancashire, we lived in a small semi-detached house which was just about big enough for mum, dad, me, older sister Elaine and young brother Christopher. I have been told that one night in the late 1950s mum, whose name was Peggy Swarbrick, went to see Marty Wilde in a Larry Parnes show at Southport. She got talking to Marty in the theatre car park and told him that if the show was ever in the Nelson area she could offer him a bed for the night as she knew that he was not well paid. She didn't think that he would take her up on the offer but left her address just in case. A few weeks later Marty's mum wrote asking if Marty and his road manager could stay overnight and that's how it all started. It was great, as I remember, my dad picking them up in our car outside the Burnley Mecca, when Marty had finished his concert, he ran through all the screaming girls and into our car.

Then, a few months later, a Larry Parnes 'roadie' named Pete Braddock, who was a very tall man, knocked on the door and asked mum if Billy Fury could stay with her but said that there was one small problem. At this point Billy bobbed his head from round the back of Pete and said that the problem was 'Crackers'. Apparently Billy had brought his boxer dog with him and asked mum if she would look after them both. Fortunately, mum was an animal lover, so 'Crackers' also stayed for lodgings. Whilst talking to Billy, Peggy found that the dog had previously belonged to Diana Dors and husband Dennis Hamilton. One day 'Crackers' was let out into the back garden of the property early in the morning to attend to a call of nature. However, being a fit and strong dog, he decided to jump over the back fence and head off across the open fields to the rear of the house. Fortunately he was obedient and came back when called but you can imagine the headlines if he had not done so! Everyone would have been in the doghouse.

The next one to stay with us was Duffy Power as it got around the Larry Parnes' boys that there was a free bed and breakfast in that area.

Looking back, the sleeping arrangements were complicated when guests stayed with us. My sister and I had a double bed in a very small room which you would call a box room now. We had to move into our parents' room and they slept downstairs on a sofa bed.

This allowed the visitors to sleep in the double bed in my tiny room. So my claim to fame is that Billy and Marty slept in my bed but unfortunately I wasn't in it at the time.

My younger sister was born on 29 January 1960. She was given the name Collette because we played Billy's record of that name to mum through the intercom as she gave birth in our front room at Nelson. My mum used to take us all over the country when the stars performed and we always got backstage to see them. I have letters from Marty's mum thanking my mother for letting him stay with us. On one occasion we went to Billy's house in Liverpool and met his mum, Jean, but Billy wasn't there at the time. One of the highlights was going to watch Marty Wilde in the Royal Command Performance at Manchester with the Queen Mother attending. I still have the programme and we managed to get backstage again to see him. My sister Elaine, whilst staying in London on a course, went to visit Marty and his wife Joyce in their flat and saw Kim who was just a baby at the time.

I went to watch the showing of the Billy Fury film 'The Sound of Fury' in Liverpool, Billy's mum and Vince Eager were there. My favourite Billy song is 'Maybe Tomorrow'. Sadly, mum, sister Elaine and brother Christopher have passed away but I will always be grateful for the fantastic memories they have left us. My son Justin is an amazing piano player with his wife Debbie being the singer in their band called 'Tipitina'. They have played at Ronnie Scotts' in London eight times and I have videos of them playing which can be seen on my Facebook wall.

Billy Fury in our back garden

Billy with 'Crackers', sister Elaine and Pete Braddock

Me on the right with sister Elaine, Marty Wilde and our young brother

12: Chris Eley

Born in Redruth in January 1949, but growing up in the very heart of rural Cornwall and living as an only child for nearly sixteen years, surrounded by farms, woods, rivers and mine burrows, and with a steam railway halt nearby, was paradise itself for a child (outside loo and adder nests excepting). Being near the cliffs, caves, and beaches of the rugged North Coast, added to the idyll and spoiled me for life for anywhere else. For adults and previous generations of all ages however, it could be a hard life.

I had a few scattered friends and cousins to play with but much of my time was spent happily alone in the countryside, with my toy guns and Butch the family mongrel. Neither property where I lived had running water until the 1970s and until the late sixties, no electricity either; something to do with wartime radio location systems. This meant a lot of reading by Calor gas light, and programmes on the accumulator radio-feeding imagination in a way regrettably almost unknown today. Reading, mostly historical works (especially from the Age of Fighting Sail), is still a primary pleasure. During my childhood and early youth World War 2 and all things American, especially westerns, were prominent and our heroes were a mix of celluloid ones (John Mills), real ones (Guy Gibson VC) or a combination of both as typified by James Stewart; film star and decorated bomber pilot. I also revered my two great uncles for their active part in the war. I believed in the heroes of the British Empire and the Old West and in a TV-less home, passed down boys' books and each new Biggles book, brought delight. Adventure, Rover, Hotspur, Wizard, and other comics and annuals added more action heroes. Brief glimpses of TV when visiting relatives or friends introduced Champion the Wonder Horse (title song performed by Frankie Laine, a favourite of young Ronnie Wycherley), life-long hero Cheyenne Bodie (Clint Walker), and others. Classic films including Ice Cold in Alex, The Man from Laramie, and later Billy Budd, Zulu, The Searchers and many more are still favourites.

Our family was not really musically inclined (unlike young Ronnie Wycherley with his mother's piano and grandma's record player), but would come to assume real importance in my life. I had heard a variety of music on the radio and TV, been taken to see the Student Prince and other music films, and I loved western themes. I recall a brief glimpse of 6.5 Special but never Oh Boy or the other TV rock programmes which followed. I had missed out on the excitement of Rock n Roll but during 1961 came to like the current sounds. I was already primed when probably around January 1962 at my maternal grandfather's home, on came All That Jazz. 'Rubbish' he snapped and the TV was turned over. However, just a few seconds of putting Billy's amazing charismatic presence together with the intense vocal that I already knew of, was a life-changing moment. From that instant I wanted, and soon tried to be, Billy Fury.

Elvis had made an impact and my belief in him possessing the most beautiful voice that I would ever hear, was clinched for me when I Can't Help Falling In Love hit the top in February of '62. Both performers became the most loved and iconic of my life but that was not to prevent me from appreciating the music of others, (whenever I discovered them), just as much. My grandfather actually liked music and had often taken us to the Cosy Nook theatre in Newquay, where I have been told Billy Fury performed either in the late sixties or seventies.

How the threads of fate play out because much later the All That Jazz performances came my way after being used, in part, in the excellent 1998 BBC TV Documentary, Halfway to Paradise. In 2007 I was able to hand the full performances over free-gratis to the lovely folk from Odeon DVD for His Wondrous Story, and again in 2015 for the No 1 DVD and TV Film Halfway to Paradise. Being invited to contribute to the films was a rare privilege.

During February 62, Letter Full of Tears made a real impression-thereafter remaining a favourite. During May, Last Night Was Made For Love typified what Billy Fury was all about, whilst the stunning King For Tonight totally blew me away (as did Jezebel by Marty Wilde that month). The real revelation however came in the July of '62 when I cycled several times in a week to the 'Flea Pit' at St Agnes to see Play it Cool. This film has been criticised for being a 'Cardboard Quickie' for inferior songs, a flimsy plot, poor acting and for Billy looking awkward. Much of that is true but I simply cannot do descriptive justice to the impact that Billy's performance presence had on me at the time. The clip from All That Jazz had been fascinating but controlled; as had any other subsequent clips I may have seen, but there was nothing restrained about some of the Fury numbers. The opening credits set the tone-riveting stuff even today, and the vocals possess a Rock n Roll and blues edge that few 'pop' singers had at the time. The Twist Kid is an amazing performance, arguably leaving even post Rock n

Roll Elvis in the shade, and whilst Shane Fenton turned in a fine performance of a number he'd written, It's Gonna Take Magic, Billy's edgy contribution takes it completely to another level. Once Upon A Dream had Billy looking cooler than he ever would again and the bluesy beginning to the end title is stunning-visually and vocally. You're Swell is a great little song-far too short, and instead of looking ungainly as sometime described, the movement of arms and those large hands only gives an extra unique, Johnnie Ray influenced edge to the performances. Hal Carter (who appeared in the film-blink and you miss him) and was later a friend to so of many of us, once told me that Billy never knew what to do with his hands. Even the subsequent Beatles earthquake lacked the effect of seeing Billy perform on screen. I soon came to like much of their music, but it would never overshadow that of my original icons. Soon I began to search out magazines, postcard sets and pictures and get clothes that resembled Billy's; but as yet I had bought no vinyl-what was the point!

It was probably in 1962 that I visited a school friend called Peter who informed me that his sister no longer wanted her records, and that I could have her Billy Fury 45s. I played them and remember saying, 'That doesn't sound like Billy, no thanks'. What a plank I was. It took me years afterwards to locate good copies of the pre-1961 singles. I just did not like the adolescent vocal, in comparison to that of 1961 onwards. Later I came to appreciate those early tracks so much more. It was during 1962 that I first heard The Sound of Fury Show on Radio Luxembourg and it was a revelation, its excellence confirmed by the essential CD release in 2005. Little wonder that I thought Billy was the best there was in the world at the time. That the masters were destroyed is a tragedy-because this surely was 'The Real Sound of Billy Fury.' Hearing songs other than known releases was marvellous, and it's sad to think that an albums worth of those tracks still remain unreleased. I remember girls travelling home on the Penwether's school bus on some Friday's, brimming with expectation. 'Guess who's on Lucky Stars tomorrow, Billy Fury' they would exclaim-and giggle. I don't recall any other solo early sixties artist eliciting such a response. Unfortunately for us all, whilst Billy came to Plymouth in 1962, he didn't seem to get to Truro.

By sometime in 1963 pop music and girls had taken over from western heroes and commandos-although air rifles and surprisingly powerful home-made nut wood long-bows would remain for quite a while! First love for an older girl, a local carnival queen, played havoc with my heart and hormones for what seemed like ages. Soon anything that reflected largely unrequited love and inevitable heartbreak, became order of the day. Like young Ronnie Wycherley's Margo, she later moved away with the love of her life. I hope she did fulfil her Nat King Cole dream and that 'It Will Be For Ever' turned out that way.

The down-side of love was so prominent in Billy's songs-in the lyrics and his highly emotive vocal delivery, that it's little wonder that the lovelorn and hurting should feel such a bond with him. I seemed to spent hours hanging over the jukebox in the Galleon Cafe, playing any record that struck a melancholy chord, especially those of Billy's. I'll Never Fall In Love Again, Somebody Else's Girl, Go Ahead And Ask Her, Do You Really Love Me Too, I Will and I'm Lost Without You, spring to mind. The great songs of others: Needles and Pins, Little Town Flirt, Tips of My Fingers (PJ Proby), I Think of You, and That Girl Belongs to Yesterday all chimed with a moping teen through those key years of '63-'65. Oddly Roy Orbison's Blue Bayou was one of the most evocative-perhaps because you felt there was a good chance the dreamer might get back to his idyll-other than only 'In Dreams'. It was perhaps fortunate that I was unaware then of Del Shannon's I Go To Pieces, or of Mr Heartbreak himself-Arthur Alexander (You Better Move On). In 1982 Billy was down to record this classic but it's likely only the backing track exists.

During 1962 and '63 it seemed Billy was neither seldom out of the charts nor off the TV and radio and despite the lack of electricity at home I bought my first record. This cost me 32/-2d (thirty two shillings and two pence) and I still have it-the incredibly diverse sixteen track 1963 LP, Billy. I placed it on my dressing table and gradually added to it when I could. In addition to the New Musical Express and magazines featuring Billy and others, I started to take Fury Monthly. My parents spent hours with me trawling around local towns, but no ocelot pattern or truly red shirt could be found. Still managing to approximate the current Fury look, I remember dancing in the Pondsmere Hotel ballroom. Susan, (a school friend), suddenly said, 'Do you know who you remind me of?' Of course I carried on French Twisting and said, 'No-who'. 'Billy Fury' she said. Well, as great moments in your life go-that's not bad-Twist Kid or what.

Going across the fields to my friend Denzel's farm house (not the famous Denzel Pemburthy should you ask), was a regular thing from years before my sixties pop awakening, so memories may be jumbled. I do seem to recall afternoon wrestling on TV, Laramie (Robert Fuller as Jess Harper was Iconic), and Thank Your Lucky Stars (TYLS) hosted by Brian Matthew just before six. With pasties and jam and cream courtesy of Denzel's generous mother, life could not have been better. Billy invariably closed TYLS with both sides of his latest release and a memorable 1963 performance indelibly imprinted was of the classic Like I've

Never Been Gone, originally a B-side in the U.S. for my friend Chase Webster (who really rates Billy, Marty and Cliff). I believe the set was a railway station but although the classic hit would become my very favourite song of all time, it was the flipside which had me practicing my moves in the bedroom mirror; What Do You Think You're Doin' Of? Written by Billy. During the intro he would clap his hands once over one shoulder, then twice over the other and there is a photo in the first TYLS book, from that performance I believe, which shows him with open fluttering hands at shoulder height during the middle-break of the number. It was just so different and not enough has been made of-the great rhythm and blues side of this performer. The only person that I recall on TYLS being striking in a similar way was Gene Vincent; clad in white leather, great presence, great voice, terrible song-Humpity Dumpity. I also remember practising bowling in my paternal grandparent's small holding yard in 1963. The kitchen window was open, Billy and The Tornados were on Saturday Club playing Sticks n' Stones, truly blissful days. On Radio Luxembourg Marty Wilde's incredible version of Lonely Avenue and Shane Fenton's Fool's Paradise really impressed but neither charted.

The popularity of such early sixties type music contrasted sharply with the events of Christmas Eve 1963, in the café by the foot of the Memorial Hall steps in Perranporth. While I was attempting to sing with Derek Lowe (guitar/vocals) and Johnny Woods (acoustic), we were forced by beat-group fans to switch from Somebody Else's Girl and Maybe Baby to the only Beatles number we knew, I Saw Her Standing There-played about three times. Even if the Derek Lowe Trio had been bursting with talent (we weren't) it was far too late to become even another Dave Lee and the Staggerlees (Cornwall's premier group), let alone another Billy Fury and Beatles. To a chorus of jeers and rolled pennies, the home made amp blew up and apart from a failed audition for the local WI Road Show, that was the end of our dreams and aspirations.

During 1964, still spending time on the small holding (they now had a generator) and at Denzel's, I recall seeing Billy miming to Nothin' Shakin' and I Will on Ready Steady Go. On Discs a Gogo I seem to remember him doing side to side leaps down a ramp before launching into Nothin' Shakin. The Billy Fury Show later that year was a big disappointment because there was so little 'Fury' in it. I do recall however thinking how cool Billy was when singing the standard, Hey Look Me Over, and a superb You Got Me Dizzy with the Gamblers. Regrettably even I knew that Billy's variety show paled beside the Granada TV Rock n Roll Show from around that time; with its three original U.S Rock n Roll greats rocking like the clappers. If Billy and the Gamblers had been included in the show; it would have been near perfect. Despite enjoying my late discovery of Rock n Roll and of new sixties beat, I still loved the really excellent 45s Billy was releasing. An eye opener that year came with the arrival of the exotic Ronettes, especially the foxy Ronnie who stirred feelings only partially awakened by other pop girls.

By the very end of 1964 I was stationed with several hundred other All Arms Junior Leaders, near Twyn in North Wales. There was only a communal TV and I remember watching Ready Steady Go as we sat around burning the pimples off our 'Ammo' boots, rubbing down the new brasses, then 'bulling' the boots. Happy days! Months later I brought my record player from home and some records. Highlights included the superb We Want Billy and The Sound of Fury albums; the Billy Fury No 2 (every track a classic), Play it Cool, Billy Fury & The Tornados and Am I Blue EPs, plus some 45s. Even today the latter EP stands out in terms of sheer blues power and excellence, especially Wondrous Place. The superb Billy Fury & The Gamblers EP, especially Turn Your Lamp Down Low, became another favourite. I had Eden Kane's first LP, the seminal Smokestack Lightnin' by Howling Wolf, various Elvis EPs and albums and the prized Come Running EP by Marty Wilde. Written by Marty, Tomorrows Clown is still one of the finest recordings ever made.

I sent off to the famous Heanor Record Centre for more Fury records and was appalled to find that those precious pre 1961 singles that I had turned down years before were now deleted. It would be years before I had a complete collection of the Decca and EMI singles. Others were playing Beatles albums and criticising my 'primitive' music choices. In Truro on leave I belatedly discovered the 1961 Halfway to Paradise LP; which for me vies with the LP Billy for top Fury album. I also obtained the 1965 I've Gotta Horse LP, but have only ever enjoyed an EPs worth of tracks. Despite featuring Billy without Fury, the film was enjoyable, but the dancing left me cold.

During early 1966 my mother stopped sending Fury Monthlies and it was to be years before I located the last handful. During 1966, I found a copy of the fantastic Donna the Prima Donna by another life-long favourite, Dion, and the classic combination of I'll Never Quite Get Over You, with the underrated and ethereal, I Belong To The Wind by Billy. Many years later an unsighted friend from the USA, Linda Gehres, described to me how having only hearing had heightened her appreciation of Billy's recordings. She felt qualified in saying that both his voice and the orchestration on tracks like the above, was so much better and infinitely more special, than any other recording artist of the era. I admit despairing when such quality singles achieved only the lower reaches of the charts. In Salisbury I picked up Billy's final 45 on Decca, Give Me Your Word, but regrettably failed to buy the Parlophone 45 that I played in the booth there, and didn't follow up on later releases. You would have thought that I would have learned my lesson from back in 1962. However, like many fans at the time, I felt it was a new sound and not the 'real' Billy Fury. Much later I came to truly appreciate those recordings in their own right.

In 1967 I served in Aden for nine months. As an eighteen year old, it was one of the most exciting and memorable periods of my whole life. On one occasion whilst on duty I was allowed to leap into the record shop in the town to pick up Billy's second LP-Billy Fury. This might have been visible through the shop window, perhaps not. Regrettably it was not a local pressing as sometimes occurred in the Middle and Far East with some releases by Billy. I also bought a Neil Sedaka hits album and I believe, The Best of Billy Fury LP, which was released that year. Ironically, whilst I was out there doing my bit, Billy with Lee Everett was in Cornwall for the Torrey Canyon oil spill disaster. During the late sixties the music press reported that Billy did an acoustic set in Redruth; but regrettably I knew nothing about it. During 1969 I saw him perform All The Way To The USA on TV, Lift Off I think.

Fast forward to 1971 and over two wonderful years spent in the Crown Colony of Hong Kong, where many days off were spent around the record stalls of Kowloon. Imagine my excitement when I first saw a copy of the 1965 London's Greatest Hitmaker's LP. What a find to hear for the very first time Billy's superb version of This Diamond Ring. Many fans knew nothing about the track until its inclusion on The World of Billy Fury Volume 2 in 1980. Billy had a few singles issued in Hong Kong, pressed locally, and although not picture cover releases, they were still collectable. Billy did apparently reach No. 1 in Singapore with It's Only Make Believe, but just one night there gave me little opportunity to search for records. In 1973 I was detached to New Zealand for six terrific weeks (it was a tough life) and I knew there would be Fury releases in that wonderful land. Could I find any-no, but years later I got hold of half a dozen 45s and an album from a source over there. Sometime during this period I joined Billy's fan club run by Tony Read. Receiving a couple of news sheets. I'm not sure just when I discovered the intriguing 1972 single, Will The Real Man Please Stand Up.

It was during 1973 that Eddie Muir, friend and editor of New Rockpile in Brighton, kindly sent me the five songs recorded by Billy on Ronco for the UK

No.1 Hit LP, That'll Be The Day. On listening to the powerful tracks my belief in Billy was reaffirmed and for the rest of my life the Billy/Elvis combination would again be the most revered musical elements in it. From 1974 I started writing to Decca with ideas or just requesting information. Later this would extend to EMI, Ronco, K-tel and even Readers Digest.

In 1974 Billy appeared for a one week stint at Talk of the West, a night club near Perranporth. Whilst on leave I discovered that Billy was appearing. The trouble was that it was the week after my leave expired and the only solution would be to go sick, which was not an option.

My collecting of Fury items had modest beginnings in 1963 but by 1966 had largely halted as my musical interests broadened and Billy faded from the charts. Rejuvenated by That'll Be The Day, from 1974 onwards I regularly spent part of my leave trawling the old record shops and resales of the Stoke on Trent, Hanley areas. Discovering the Discs A Gogo EP for fifty pence, and hearing Don't Walk Away for the first time was an amazing experience. In 1974 I bought the catchy new single on Warner Brothers, I'll Be Your Sweetheart, but it was the B-side I really enjoyed, Fascinating Candle Flame, written by Billy. I read that an album was to follow and that Billy had recorded Jackson Brown's These Days. I waited in vain for months for those still missing recordings.

Being in Berlin during 1976/77, (where I could only find the German Decca red label equivalent of The World of Billy Fury), I missed out on the first Russell Harty Show featuring Billy. Seeing Chuck Berry (on form) and the Rolling Stones (mind-blowing) helped to make up for it. In a Stoke record shop during 1979 I bought, from the famous and hirsute 'Legendary Lonnie' (of Screaming Lord Sutch's Savages fame), the disappointing but welcome Golden Years LP. Hal Carter later told me that he hated it but at least it gave us some hits in stereo. I do recall seeing a black and white advert for the album on TV in Stoke, but an attempt to locate the on-stage jumpsuit footage failed. We have of course seen similar footage whilst watching Halfway to Paradise, The Billy Fury Story show with Colin Gold and Fury's Tornados; whose more than twenty year promotion of Billy's music has been a very positive thing, along with Gavin Stanley, Michael King and others. It was whilst living in Sussex during the late seventies that I built up my music collection, with trips to the dealers' shops in Brighton.

In 1980, whilst at Warton, I wrote to Billy care of a record dealer I knew, enquiring about rare acetates and the likelihood of future Fury recordings. There was no reply but I carried on collecting and writing again to Decca about future releases. It was from the seventies to the mid-nineties that John Tracy brought out some classic music releases, often featuring unreleased tracks and versions. He later found several unreleased recordings for an anthology he wanted to do and told me of them. Regrettably he left before the project could be started and in 1997/98 I was fortunate to be able to compile and annotate the release for Deram. In 1981 in Catterick I got wind of a new Billy Fury single, the first really new recording since 1974. I drove to Harrogate, picked up three copies, and played both terrific sides to death. The excellent 45, wrong key notwithstanding, came in a classy hard cardboard blue cover, and contained a sixties sounding Be Mine Tonight coupled with No Trespassers. It stalled just outside of the Top 100. I can't describe the sheer joy that release bought and with it, such hope for the future.

In February of 1982 I went to my first Elvis event because Billy was rumoured to be attending. During the day at Wembley, Alvin Stardust and others were warmly welcomed, but when Billy walked on the place erupted, with fans rushing to the foot of the stage. He was wearing the Be Mine Tonight picture single outfit and his presence was incredible. Acknowledging the applause he was perhaps about to speak when a young male fan, totally carried away, jumped on stage nearly knocking him over. This was unsurprising as Billy was really thin, and according to the stage manager (when I asked him beforehand if I could get backstage), had had half a bottle of whiskey poured down him, just to get him to walk on, he was that apprehensive. The fan himself tripped and fell, picked himself up, handed his camera to a bemused Tony Prince and posed with Billy. Unsurprisingly Billy had had enough, and with a wave, walked off. I didn't get a photo or backstage, which was a great pity after twenty years of near worship

On 4th March that year Billy collapsed at Rhos Farm in Mid-Wales and thanks to partner Lisa made it to hospital in London just in time. The report in the press showed a recovering Billy in bed, so I sent a get well card and a reply arrived from Billy's then manager, Tony Read. In July there was a mention in the Sun that Billy was possibly to appear at the Blue Boar site near Hucknall. A teenage fan called Ian Proctor had already picked up many of the Fury rarities before I arrived, but I bought some nice items and became acquainted with Tony Read. Later that afternoon, Billy arrived in a mustard coloured Range Rover. He was wearing an owl T-shirt and I asked Tony if I could have it when Billy tired of it. He gave it to me in the summer of 1983, and it has been my most treasured possession ever since; although I had not wanted to acquire it that way. I enjoyed seeing Marty Wilde perform for the first time but the later performances over ran. The Stargazers were still on when it was time for Billy and it was rumoured that he would not now appear. It was to be his first full gig since 1976/77 and I knew from February that his nerves would be in shreds. Fans were filled with trepidation.

When Billy eventually appeared I was fourteen again and too in awe to record each song but I seem to think that first came the strains of Wondrous Place and the sight of Billy's back, until he turned and powerfully delivered the rest of the 1960 classic. What followed was a mix of rockers and old ballad hits, all with the loud and punchy guitar of the late Mick Green. At one point near the beginning Billy sang the words to a totally different song, sheepishly apologising, but no one cared. He sounded good and looked it too. Suddenly my always being in the wrong place at the wrong time over the years was no bad thing, allowing this to be an ultimate moment. Only two worthwhile photos of mine really came out from that night and someone was recording on a hand-held cassette, which has not yet come to light. It would be good to confirm the track running order; Say Mama probably being a figment of my imagination.

During the summer I stayed overnight at Tony's Dorset farm house, expecting Billy to turn up as had been hinted at, but no such luck. Tony was planning an EP with Decca (mainly to release My Christmas Prayer again), and asked me which track I would like included. I asked for You're Having The Last Dance With Me, and was surprised later when it was featured. I did get hold of one of the promotional 'Ice Cream' shirts that Billy apparently didn't like; white with a green Polydor logo, and posters of Love or Money, the new 45. These large posters were partly luminous and with rather clever innuendo proclaimed Billy Fury's Back, with a silhouette of his back and the song title. I took a few and had them placed in record shops from Cornwall and Stoke to Yorkshire. For years, one of them was displayed at Billy Fury weekends in Blackpool.

My next involvement was going down to Burton-on-Trent Inde Coope Social Club on 1st October. Many of the fans, including the 'Nottingham Girls' who had been at Hucknall, were in attendance, and it was a great night. Whilst the first outfit of red leather trousers, red boots (why did I once say pink) and white sleeveless Tee shirt with red 'Love or Money' hearts and pound signs motifs, may not have been what some fans would have preferred, the performance was memorable, especially in the delivery of Unchain My Heart and My Babe. Later in the evening Billy wore black leather trousers with flowered shirt, and played acoustic guitar. He delivered Love or Money, not an easy number to master, and ended with Johnny B Goode. Afterwards I met him for a photograph, being one of the first in line, together with a Billy pen friend, young Jerry Vincent from

London. Billy was absolutely exhausted and should not have been kept standing for so long, waiting for fans who were queuing the length of the premises to meet him. When I asked if anyone had a more user friendly camera than the one handed to me by Jerry, Billy growled, 'You mean like an instamatic'. I was holding things up and acutely nervous but things were different at our second meeting. Afterwards Tony handed me a box of Polydor 45s to sell in the club, and I had the kick of being part of the organisation for the evening. I met great friend to be Frank Bull at the event and young Jerry, with his street savvy and rockers quiff, got taken on as part of the team.

Work issues made me miss attending the Beck Theatre show, but on December 4th I managed to get down to The Sunnyside Hotel in Northampton for the second gig there. Billy was tanned, looked great and sounded better than before, partly due to a more sympathetic young band, The Four Aces, and also perhaps because he was far more relaxed and treating the gig as a party, down to hoovering drinks off the tables. The night was recorded by Jerry and myself, and later saw a release on an Ozit label CD, The Last Concert. I again met Billy, he was placed behind a table and I didn't feel that I could ask if I could stand next to him for a shot. A nice fan, June I think, was in shot when the photo was taken by someone. Jerry introduced me as the guy who had been networking with some fans, putting up posters, and helping at the Burton gig. Billy said, 'Thanks Lah for what you do' and could not have been nicer. I gave him the choice of two photos I had taken at Hucknall. Smiling he chose the obviously best one, quite an iconic shot used in the 2018 Biography Halfway to Paradise, (written by those nice folk Caroline and David Stafford), signing the other one for me. It was this encounter, with Billy being so gracious and a perfect gent, that primarily made me agree to be a founder member of the Sound of Fury Fan club in 1996. Wondrous Face by Liverpool's Spencer Leigh, although less sympathetic than the above, is also essential reading. The Worldwide Discography by fan Peter Baldia from Vienna, complements the biographies. Tony Read had already asked me to write a 'book' (he meant tour brochure for 1983), yet didn't want me to interview Billy. We disagreed over this after the Sunnyside and sadly I had nothing more to do with Billy's engagements from that point. Work reasons later prevented me from attending the subsequent funeral, always a source of deep regret to me.

On 28 January 1983 around 2pm Ian Proctor phoned me at work in tears. Billy had died. It was a truly crippling, almost physical blow, of the kind that is felt when a very close friend dies, even though sadly he wasn't. Although we all knew Billy had a heart problem, he had looked so fit in December that this tragic news was unexpected to us, although not to those close to him. When Elvis died it had been a massive shock, partly because, selfishly, I realised that it was the end of the regular album injection of great new songs that had sustained me up to 1977, and should have been able to for another thirty years! With Billy it was not only the loss of future recordings but personal more than anything. I had met him, the kindred countryside loving, loner spirit, and the primary figure to induce in me a love of music. Like everyone else I have stark memories of the TV and newspaper coverage of Billy's death and funeral service. To see him prematurely robbed, not only of a successful comeback, but his life, has always been the source of deepest sadness.

In March '83 I bought the hastily compiled but excellent LP, The One And Only, and in May, the beautiful single, Forget Him. It played Let Me Go Lover so of course I took it back, not to exchange but to see if there were any more. Regrettably there were none. Tony later informed me that Polydor had planned the old Kathy Kirby hit to be a single release but pulled it in favour of Forget Him, which he preferred. Allegedly two hundred and fifty copies of Let Me Go Lover had been pressed but how may faulty copies of Forget Him there were, no one knows!

In the summer of 1983, I visited Tony's home once more. A bedroom was full of Billy's clothing, much of it dry cleaned and hanging up, the rest on the bed. He said, 'Take what you want'. Perhaps foolishly I couldn't face rooting around in Billy's possessions, saying just give me something nice. Regrettably only a very few items sold to me had visual evidence of Billy wearing it. Most of the stuff has gone now, auctioned for the Bronze Fund, raffled, sold and in several cases, given to deserving fans and friends, including tribute acts. The Aladdin Panto black stage suit (with photo) is on loan to the British Music Experience in Liverpool.

I believe gatherings at Mill Hill Cemetery began in 1983 and resulted in some fans being invited back to the late Frank Bull's Enfield flat. The much-missed Frank soon arranged for the Sunday hire of a Mill Hill Church Hall in nearby Salcombe Gardens, where for years we all attended twice annually, until Billy's Mum Jean suggested it to be three times a year. Hal Carter was a welcome regular (he brought Eden Kane once) but sadly visits by such original celebrities were few. That made the appearance of Billy's contemporaries, such as our great friends, Danny Rivers and the recently deceased Peter Wynn, that much more special. For years now the venue has been St Paul's Church Hall up on the nearby Ridgeway.

It was in 1983 that Alan and Carol Chapman formed The Fury Sound, tastefully running it into the 1990s, producing some good magazines for the time, assisting with the release of unreleased material, and helping fans fill gaps in their record collections.

Around 1986 or so Frank Bull, Hal Carter, and Billy's Mum, with friends of theirs such as Maureen Bowden, Jackie Clark, and Rita Smalley began the process of upgrading Billy's memorial. Permission to have a marble surround and photographs on the headstone was obtained from the grave owners, the Rosen family. The grave has been looked after by Billy's fans (Frank and then the Sound of Fury), on behalf of the Billy Fury Estate ever since. Damage has been repaired and pictures replaced. Today ownership still resides with Billy's former long-term partner, our Patron Lisa Voice, who has recently paid for cleaning, restoration and improvements, including cobalt blue chippings. The SOF, with the help of local fans, still monitors and liaises with the estate when necessary. Worthy of note is that Billy's old rocker mate Danny Rivers, and lovely wife Emily, (a dancer in Summer Holiday) lie buried just down the road in Hendon Cemetery.

The wooden seat opposite Billy's grave was placed shortly after his death by a few fans and the family, being replaced by the Sound of Fury during the 2000s. In 1991 the Billy Fury Tribute Weekends started in Blackpool at the Carousel Hotel and in 1992 I attended with Frank Bull. We ended up driving Billy's Mum around to record shops and at the event I met Linda, the special lady who eventually became my partner, sustaining and supporting my Billy Fury endeavours (and my life). Blackpool Weekends run by Diane and Mrs Roth, together with incredible singer and good friend Colin Paul, have been a regular event ever since. Their prolonged contribution to the subsequent Bronze Fund was one of the most significant of all. Many other performers have also become good friends and include Graham Hunter, Johnny Red, Rob Dee, Alan Wilcox, Roger Sea, Colin Gold, Peter Williams, Alan French and the late Brian Lee among others.

Despite losing Billy, the years up to 1997 were good and harmonious ones for fans, lacking the pressures that would soon follow. We were a small, (until 1991 at least) devoted band around Billy's Mum, the focal point right up until her death in 2017 for many fans. In June 1993 I spent several hours with her at 'Wondrous Place' where I was shown her photo albums, saw Billy's two Silver Discs and held the famous Carl Alan Award. In July she sent me a nice letter which mentions Mick Hill's Billy Fury Appreciation Society, so perhaps the Fury Sound had finished by then. I had once been, at a Paul Neon Billy Fury gig, asked by close friends of Billy's Mum to form a fan club on her behalf but declined because of the existence of the Fury Sound. In the event Alan and Carol retired and the short-lived society folded. Sometime in the early nineties I attended a charity night in Liverpool featuring Billy's brother, Albie, who became more involved in fan events from 1997 onwards, and helped, with Jean, to raise funds for the Bronze Fund.

During 1996, six of us Mill Hill regulars decided to get together and form The Sound of Fury (SOF) Syndicate, Maureen Bowden, Jackie Clark, Jean Prosser, Clare Mehmet-Nugent, Mick Hill and myself. Lisa Voice graciously gave us her blessing. Our first magazine came out in early 1997, our last in December 2018. Finnish fan Nalle Westman, with our help, created an award winning Billy Fury website. The results of our purely voluntary efforts can be found in our sixty two magazines, other publications, on the internet, and in the numerous CD and DVD film releases worked on since our formation. For me it was always about the music. Perhaps more than anything else, our successful managing and delivering, with Peter and Lynda Keller, of their wonderful Bronze Statue Project, realised by sculptor Tom Murphy, will be testament to the achievement of everyone involved the six SOF syndicate members, several hundred fan club general members (at the time there was only the Sound of Fury in the UK), and all other parties involved. Our early magazines tell the story of those key venue owners, performers, fans and others who helped us raise the funding. From memory I must mention the incredibly generous Ian and (the late) Sheila Alexander, daughter Sam and all attending their Allendale Hotel during the crucial miniature statue stage, Mark Wilsmore and all performing and attending the Ace Cafe, the gracious Janet Dugdale and team at the museum of Liverpool, and Moya Gleave of the NZ Fan Club. Also Vince Eager and Harry Whitehouse of billyfury.com, without either of whom there would have been no Jack Good to lend credibility to the unveiling day. For Mo Bowden and me, writing the statue plaque and being invited to speak on the day were unbelievable honours.

Mick Hill sadly died before Tom Murphy's excellent bronze of Billy was completed, but his work with us and in his Rock You Sinners magazines still lives on. Clare Mehmet-Nugent was unable to attend the unveiling day, leaving us and doing another splendid job in diabetes awareness circles before succumbing to an illness. Indomitable treasurer Jean Prosser (with husband Mike) put together one final magazine and retired. The irrepressible Mo Bowden, with her front row memories of Billy in 1959, also left in 2003 and the democratic syndicate became a team. Replacements Jenny Warwick, (then owner of Rhos Farm) and Vic England left to create The Billy Fury In Thoughts Of You Fan Club, with life-long fan Peter (scribe from the North) Davies and wife Jen taking their places in the firing line. The now long-serving SOF venue and magazine stalwarts, Ken and Cecilia Darvell, ace treasurer Wendy Wright (supported by husband Phil), myself (supported by partner Linda Shawley), and our quiet mannered and dedicated secretary, Jackie Clark, all continue to do our best to promote Billy. This is currently done via the newsletter, (produced by modest and talented Lee Fry, a significant internet Fury presence in his own right), future (we hope) music releases, at venues (when we can) and our website, Harry Whitehouse's former and excellent billyfury.com, now run by our friend Alan Coombe. A detailed account of events following Billy's passing could fill a book, the first tribute concert, music releases, Billy Fury Memorial Fund, the myriad tribute acts, bands and stage shows, individual fans charitable works, the Fury Sound, billyfury.com/peaksoft and BFITOY Fan Club achievements, the Bronze Project story, Liverpool Cathedral Lectern, Lisa's Cavendish Avenue Blue Plaque event and more.

The 'Billy' friends we have made have enriched our lives but far too many have been lost, the single worst aspect of it all. Fans have gathered at the statue since 2003, in addition to the Fury weekends 'Up North' but gathering at Billy's resting place has always been special somehow, even if it can only be for a very few hours, and for a limited number. Dedicated Mill Hill regulars from all over the UK, have long been among the most loyal of fans and hopefully can continue to be, fate permitting. Certainly, fans will be visiting Billy's resting place for years to come, especially as younger music fans come to discover a true British music legend. Billy really has impacted our lives, and not only whilst he was with us!

Chris Eley

Chris in the Derek Lowe Trio 1963/4.

Billy at Euston Station during filming of 'Play it Cool'

Relaxing on location for the same film

Studying the script on location at Euston Station

On Thank Your Lucky Stars, probably 1962

Chris finally meets Billy at Burton on Trent

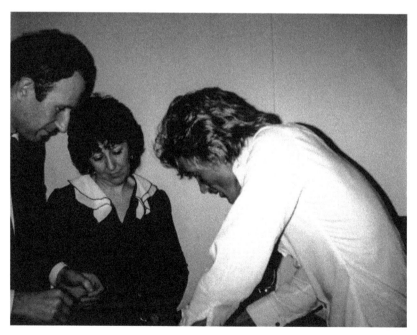

Billy, June and Chris at The Sunnyside Hotel, Northampton

All seven pictures are copyright to Chris Eley

13: Christine Newton and Michael Parkinson

Whilst preparing for a Billy Fury Dance show, to be performed at the Mansfield Palace Theatre on 8 October 2011, Mr Roy Newton telephoned me. He explained that he had bought tickets for the show as a present for his wife whose birthday was a week later. He went on to tell me about why his wife was a keen Billy Fury fan and told me a story which impressed me so much that I decided to include it in the show. Roy and I decided that we would make it a surprise for Christine so she knew nothing about it until her story was read by one of the narrators in the show and I presented her with a DVD of the film. This is what happened.

The story of watching Billy Fury filming 'I've Gotta Horse' in 1964

I was staying in a caravan, on holiday, at a site at Caister-on-Sea, in Norfolk with my parents, Dorothy and Thomas Peck.

On Monday 24th September 1964 we went to a horse-riding stables (after a lot of pestering on my part). Unfortunately, there was no riding that day as the stables had been loaned to a film crew who were filming 'I've Gotta Horse' featuring Billy Fury, The Bachelors and Leslie Dwyer.

We were allowed to stay and watch the filming, and have our pictures taken with the cast, as they wanted to keep it a secret and didn't want us to going off and telling other people.

Also during the holiday (I think the same day as the filming) we went to see the Billy Fury Show at a theatre in Great Yarmouth (I think it was the Britannia Theatre). We went in to Great Yarmouth early so that we could have some tea first and, when we got there, fire engines were just roaring up to the Theatre. At first we thought the theatre was on fire and the show would be cancelled but then we saw they were filming again.

My married name is Mrs Christine Newton but I was Christine Peck then and it was six weeks before my fifteenth birthday.

Whilst compiling this book I decided to include this story but could not contact Christine on the telephone number that I had for them so I made a request to Radio Nottingham to try to locate her or Roy. They invited me to speak 'on air' with presenter Alan Clifford on Friday 22 January but despite our best efforts I could not establish contact.

Christine with Billy Fury, apologies for the quality of these pictures

Billy with dad

Mother with Con Cluskey

Mum with Dec and Con Cluskey and John Stokes (the Bachelors)

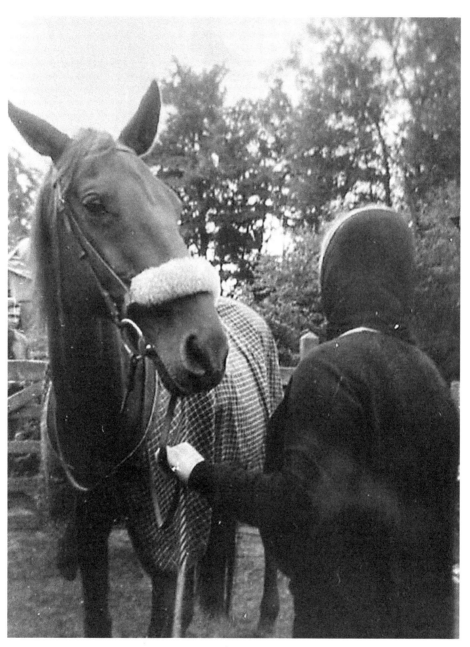

Anselmo, Billy Fury's Horse

14: COLIN PAUL

I was born in the summer of 1962, at the height of Billy Fury's popularity so it wasn't for another 14 years that I would soon discover our very own home grown icon. When I was eight in 1970 I discovered the music of Elvis Presley when I first heard 'The Wonder of You' and upon hearing that voice I knew it was gonna be a life long adventure. The more I discovered about Elvis and his music the more I wanted to discover about his contemporaries. In 1976 I saw a picture that would have a lasting effect on my life...it was Elvis and a guy who looked similar yet different in his own way. It was in a fan club magazine 'The Elvis Monthly'. The photo was of Elvis and, as I would soon discover, Billy Fury. I didn't have a clue who he was yet I was drawn to the photo and on a mission to find out more. The article in the monthly was of course about the famous meeting on the set of Elvis's movie 'Girls, Girls, Girls', and where Billy saw Elvis record two songs... the 1962 UK Christmas Number 1 of 'Return to Sender' and of course the fantastic 'Because of Love' that Billy loved and couldn't wait to get back to the UK to record it.

Billy Fury. I remember thinking at 14 years of age WOW what a cool name, who is this man? I did my research which was very minimal in those days, no internet, pop music channels etc, just good ol' Radio Luxembourg and my local record shop. I couldn't wait to visit and, with my pocket money I had been saving up, I went along to find as much music as I could of Mr Fury. Bear in mind at this point I hadn't even heard what he sounded like, did he sound like Elvis? I soon discovered absolutely not, this was another guy in a class of his own. As I looked through the albums in the store I reached F and searched through looking for anything Fury and there it was this great Rock n Roll face looking at me. I could see not one but two albums staring at me as though to say, here I am buy me. The two albums I recall were 'Billy' and a rather smaller album... 'The Sound of Fury'. Unfortunately I only had enough for one album. Which one do I buy, oh no I thought which one? I vaguely remember asking the guy behind the counter which one should I buy as I could only afford one. He was amused at the fact that I was buying a Billy album as I had told him I've never heard him sing plus the fact that it wasn't Elvis, as it was always Elvis he said. I told him the story about reading my Elvis Monthly and reading all about Billy and he only comes from down the road I said. I was in my home town of Manchester and Liverpool isn't far away. I think he said he lives in London now or thereabouts, but I don't remember much more about the conversation, but I do remember I had enough money to buy The 'Sound of Fury' and the latest Elvis single 'Suspicion' a re-release from the early sixties but I had never heard it before. I told the guy in the record store I'd be back soon for the other Billy album. I rushed home and put the album on my record player that my parents had bought me the Christmas before, hoping it would play as it was smaller than all my Elvis albums. What happened next absolutely floored me. What the hell is that sound. I loved the echo effect of Billy's voice and as we all now know and I later found out it was a take on getting the old Memphis Sun Sound in the UK. At that time I didn't even know what the Sun Sound was. As far as I knew the sun was in the sky and that was that. I absolutely loved it and believe me it didn't take long to wear that album out. I still have it but I daren't try to play it. I asked my parents about Billy and they told me how popular he was and all about his songs including 'Halfway to Paradise',... er Halfway to where? There was so much I had to learn and I knew that I would learn one way or another.

It took me another few weeks before I had enough money to buy the other album, I rushed back to the store and it was closed, oh no I remember thinking then realised it was lunch time. All stores closed for lunch back then. I'm not sure what I did whether I went to the park or back home but I do remember going back later in the afternoon and yes it was open. I quickly rushed over to the album section and under F, oh no it wasn't there, it's gone, I looked through some other categories like B for 'Billy', but no the album wasn't there. Then I felt a tap on my shoulder the guy who served me previously (unfortunately I can't remember his name) smiled at me and said is this what you're looking for? It was 'Billy', I couldn't believe it. He had actually put it behind the counter for me, not only that but he had two singles, the before mentioned 'Halfway to Paradise' and 'I'd Never Find Another You'. I was a few new pence too short, it didn't matter because it turned out the owner was a big Billy fan and he let me off, saying to know that someone my age just 14 in 1976 liked bloody good music.

The store was in my home town of Sale and changed hands a few times in the eighties before finally closing down, but what great memories I have of visiting that record shop to build up my ever growing Billy Fury record collection.

Still in 1976 I couldn't believe how smooth Billy's voice was on all four songs of these two singles and all 16 songs from 'Billy' the album. The next album I purchased was the 'We Want Billy' album. To hear him sing live was fantastic and through the years I wanted more and I got it all.

Around 1978/9 I saw a TV advert for an album it was Billy singing his greatest hits, I couldn't grasp at first that they were re-recordings for K-TEL. Billy recorded these after striking a deal with the record company after going into bankruptcy. It was great to see Billy on the TV. This was the first time for me, being born later and missing all those wonderful 'Oh Boy' and 'Ready Steady Go' shows amongst others.

By now I was working and I could afford any Elvis or Billy release I wanted.

With my old record store being under new management in 79 and going more in the punk rock direction, I had to go to Stretford for the latest albums plus a great Golden Oldies section. Funny enough the record store was right opposite the Stretford Essoldo where Billy performed his first show outside his home town of Liverpool. But at this point in time I didn't have a clue, as far as I knew it was a Bingo Hall. So what!

I walked in the store in Stretford after work and there it was.. the K-TEL album on a stand staring out at me. What a great feeling that was. I bought it and couldn't wait to get home and play it, even though I had heard all the songs before, but hey they were new recordings and that's great with me.

In 1982 I was twenty years old and I wanted a pop career of my own. Little did I know at the time that the connection between Elvis, Billy and myself would grow even closer. I also discovered Billy had a farm in South Wales and I was determined I was gonna meet him as my dream to meet Elvis died along with him in 1977. Alas, fate was to step in once again and crush that dream. In June of 1982 after singing in my local pub I decided to put myself out there and sing my fave Rock n Roll songs to a wider audience than just my local. I was so shy in those days and let's say I always needed a little Dutch courage for the first few months. I surprised myself how much I had achieved already as I really was such a shy teenager and now at twenty I was determined my shyness wasn't gonna hold me back any longer. No more practising in front of the mirror in my bedroom to 'Halfway to Paradise' and more, it was time to get out there. I auditioned for several clubs and managed to get myself some bookings. My diary was filling up nicely and at the time I was working in a supermarket stacking shelves and training to be a store manager, but deep down that's not what I really wanted to do, although I did achieve it for a short while. No, I had a bigger agenda and as my shyness started to disappear and my confidence started to grow I really started to grow on the Manchester cabaret scene and to see the smile on the audience face when I sang a Billy song was incredible. I didn't drive in those early days and my Dad (Paul McGrath) drove me to my gigs. I have to say though even though I was a massive Elvis and Billy fan my first hero and inspiration was my Dad. He too was a singer in the local clubs and pubs as well as being a top end mechanic, but I wanted more.

When Billy passed away in January 1983 I was devastated to say the least. I couldn't believe it. Another hero gone, yet he was so much closer than Memphis and I could have got to meet him but didn't. My connection with Billy was all over or was it?

I continued throughout the eighties to further and grow my career and in 1988 I advertised for musicians to form a band. It all happened very quickly and 'The Stormbeats' were soon on the road doing Billy proud. We became Manchester Band of the Year on several occasions. We were invited to play on a Billy Fury tribute weekend in Blackpool in February 1992, it was the second event held at the Carousel Hotel, owned by Mrs June Roth and her daughter Diane Wardle who still host the Billy weekends today but now at the Metropole Hotel. The weekend was a great success then a few weeks later out of the blue we received a call from a guy called Albert Wycherley. He wanted us to perform on a show in Liverpool at The Montrose Club. It was a special Billy Fury charity night. We jumped at the chance, but hold on, Wycherley that's Billy's surname, are you a relative of Billy's we asked, Yes I'm his brother and I'll be hosting the show. I couldn't believe it we were gonna meet a family member and he is hosting the show. Then we found out he would be singing too, backed by a band called 'The Dions', a very popular Liverpool band,

'The Undertakers' were on the show and the compere was Radio Merseyside's Frankie Conner. Albie would be singing his brother's songs and he wanted us to perform songs by other Rock n Roll artistes of the era. We were made up and couldn't wait.

Well the day had arrived and so had we at the club, a little early I might add, and very excited. We met Albie who introduced us to his and Billy's Mam ...The Duchess Mrs. Jean Wycherley. I couldn't believe it. It really was like meeting Rock n Roll royalty. The show was a great success and we went on to play many more of these special shows. Albie and I hit it off straight away and we became great friends, He talked many times of his love and affection for his brother. I learned a lot about Billy through Albie and Jean and as our friendships grew

111

Albie confided in me about a lot of things and we spent many nights on the phone putting the world to rights. I got myself a new band.... Colin Paul and The Persuaders and now all these years later we are still going strong and paying our tribute to Billy when and wherever we can. The tradition at The Carousel Hotel continued and Diane Wardle continued to book The Persuaders on the now famous Billy Fury weekends only this time we backed Albie on stage and what a pleasure that was and those memories remain etched in my brain and heart. I was also offered several summer seasons at the Carousel performing my solo show. Albie and sometimes Jean would come along and support me, I always persuaded (pardon the pun) Albie to join me onstage for a few numbers then after the show we would hit the bars and restaurants and have a bloody good night out on the town. Since the early days of working in a supermarket I had changed jobs several times before going professional with my singing career, from swimming instructor to private detective a job I really enjoyed.

Albie discovered my other living and asked me to help him on a private matter. I agreed and we went on a little journey one night to sort out the problem. It was dealt with and we both ended up at Jean's for supper. Jean wasn't only The Duchess but as anyone knows whoever visited she was the perfect hostess and before you had even sat down the sandwiches, cakes and tea were on the table. On several occasions Jean let me tour the house that Billy had bought for her in 1960 (Wondrous Place) to see all of Billy's awards, from the likes of the New Musical Express and Variety Club, amongst others, was an absolute delight. Hundreds of family photos of Billy growing up and of course many from his career. I felt I knew him in a sense. Albie booked 'The Persuaders' and me on a local TV Show in Liverpool. We really enjoyed that. The show was called Billy and Wally's night out and clips can be seen on YouTube. Albie had just recorded 'Helpless' at the time and to me it's the best song he ever recorded. He sounds so much like Billy on that song and it was great to see him shine once more. Most of you will know that Albie had a successful singing career himself in the sixties firstly under the name of Al Trent then Jason Eddie and The Centre men. He had a couple of chart hits and recorded for that great producer of the sixties Joe Meek. We often discussed his career and Albie admitted as much as he idolised and loved his brother it was hard living in his shadow.

In 2008 Albie wanted to record some of his brother's hits and some of his favourite Elvis songs. So I took my recording equipment to his house and we produced plenty of material that later formed two albums, they were 'Albie sings Elvis' that was released shortly after the session. It sold very well at his concerts and the album 'Heart and Soul' a compilation of some of his early songs mixed in with the Billy songs came out after Albie passed away in tribute to Albie and his musical career.

I also have recordings of Albie rehearsing with 'The Persuaders' unreleased at this time.

The Fury weekends in Blackpool continued and it got so big that we changed it from once a year to twice a year and now at the larger hotel The Metropole Hotel. The weekends are held in March and November every year. The highlight for many years was always the fact the both Jean and Albie were there for the weekend and everyone loved to see Albie perform his tribute to Billy. It couldn't get better than that. In 2000 and 2001 we were booked along with Albie to do two concerts at the famous Winter Gardens in Blackpool and a run of shows in London, all a success and a company I work for called 'Yesterday Once More' booked Albie and the band to play at holiday camps in Southport and Brean Sands Holiday Park. All sell out shows and an absolute pleasure. As the years rolled by Albie became ill and it was apparent he was having lung, heart and kidney problems, I remember Albie telling me that he along with Billy had Rheumatic fever as a kid and I let him know that I too suffered from that disease when I was 7 years old, lucky for me it didn't leave me with a bad heart.

On 5 September 2011 Albie passed away peacefully in hospital aged just 68.

The only comfort being that he was reunited with his lovely wife Marie who passed away a few years earlier and of course with Billy and his father Albert. Once again Jean was left heartbroken. To lose not one but two sons was just too much to bear. Many of Jean's friends and what was left of her family gathered around her and surrounded her with all the love and care that they could.

In November of 2011 we paid a special tribute to Albie at the Blackpool weekend, but it just didn't feel the same without him. Our DJ, the ever popular Neil Williams, featured Albie on the big screen and showed one of his concerts. The weekend was dedicated to his memory. Jean was in attendance, all I can remember is how hard it must have been for her to be there, yet she said she wanted to as it gave her comfort and the fans would help her come to terms with her loss. What an amazing lady. I remember 'The Persuaders' and me taking to the stage and while playing our Billy set I found myself looking in the wings as if I was looking out for Albie to come and join us on stage. We too paid tribute and when it came to singing 'Helpless' everyone was in tears and that's exactly how we felt.

In 2012 The Persuaders and I took our Billy Fury show to the theatre and quickly realised we could do a double show and call it 'A Tale of Two Kings'. Obviously the show was dedicated to Billy and Elvis and became a great success. We also had onstage backing singers 'The Passionettes' and we invited dancers to each show to join the show while having both Billy and Elvis on the big screen behind us. Through modern technology I even managed to duet with Billy on 'Nobody's Child'.

The tribute shows to Billy kept coming as did several TV appearances and documentaries. Jean was always in attendance and continued to join in the fun especially in Blackpool and we were very well looked after by the 'Billy Fury In Thoughts of You' fan club hosts. The fan club was set up a few years earlier by both Jean and Albie.

As the years rolled by we had many more occasions to celebrate and one being Jean's 90th birthday. We held a party for her at The Metropole and everyone had a great time. The band and I played her favourite songs 'In Thoughts of You, Lady and Helpless'. She even joined us on stage. Jean continued to attend the weekends even when it was apparent she was unwell and her age was taking its toll on her, but to Jean she didn't care she just wanted to be at any Billy event for the fans. Her final public appearance was in Blackpool in March 2017 and on 17 May of that year Jean passed away and joined her husband Albert and her two famous sons for eternity. Jean's funeral was held at St Anne's Church Aigburth on Thursday 25 May. It was a lovely service and one of the hardest things I have ever done in my life was to sing our song 'In Thoughts of You' at the service.

I say our song as we often sang it together either in Blackpool or at the fan club meetings in Blundell St Liverpool. Again if you search YouTube there are many clips of us singing together and I will treasure those memories forever. When I was asked to sing at Jean's funeral, I didn't hesitate I just said yes straight away, it was the right thing to do and my way of saying thank you not only to Jean but to both Billy and Albie for the great memories and career that I had and continue to have. I will forever be in their debt as I truly believe they helped shape who I am. I was very honoured and proud that Jean said, publicly and privately on many occasions, that she regarded me as her third son. That is truly an honour. I have been blessed to perform so many great songs that Billy recorded here is a list of some of my favourites I like to perform and why:-

MAYBE TOMORROW – with this being his first pro recording it just has to be included here. A great 50's love song and so loved by many today whether you're a fan of Billy's or not. Such a great smooch love song.

LIKE IV'E NEVER BEEN GONE – for the simple reason his many fans all over the world will never let him go and quite rightly to.

I'D NEVER FIND ANOTHER YOU – such a great early sixties pop song to sing. It's as simple as that.

CROSS MY HEART – always a fan favourite and a dance floor filler.

STAND BY ME – for the same reason as above except for the fact you sing along with this and it will be in your head all day. From Billy's second movie, I've Gotta Horse.

TURN YOUR LAMP DOWN LOW – a song way ahead of its time.

FIND OUT WHAT'S HAPPENING – Billy's version is such a funky song to sing and dance to.

DON'T KNOCK UPON MY DOOR – simply because it's a piece of classic British Rock n Roll

RUNNING AROUND – a dance floor filler that's been kind to me over the years.

RUN TO MY LOVING ARMS – a most haunting ballad and so great to sing.

IN THOUGHTS OF YOU – treasured memories of singing with Jean.

A THOUSAND STARS – a real fifties crooner that brings back lots of special memories of family and friends I have lost over the years.

I'M LOST WITHOUT YOU – this has to be my favourite Billy song to sing. A very powerful and meaningful song of lost love that really tells a story and pulls on the old heartstrings.

HALFWAY TO PARADISE – Billy's anthem and most famous song, brings back great memories of Albie and Jean on stage together with the band singing it loud and proud encouraging the audience to join in, not that they need much encouraging.

I'LL NEVER QUITE GET OVER YOU – another excuse to sing such a powerful and emotional song.

MY ADVICE – British Rockabilly at its very best. Billy proved that you don't have to be American to sing and play Rock n Roll, also means so much to me, as stated earlier, it was featured on the first Billy album I bought and wore out.

I'LL SHOW YOU – brings back great memories of buying the Billy album and the Albie Wycherley recording session at his home in Wavertree, Liverpool

I LOVE HOW YOU LOVE ME – the same reasons as above and my wife's (Sarahlea) favourite Billy Fury recording.

WONDROUS PLACE – always have such a wonderful time on stage with this one, especially in the old days when I could mimic Billy with his cigarette and hat, not forgetting the lovely dancers who accompanied me.

ONCE UPON A DREAM – a beautiful love song from Billy's first feature film 'Play it Cool'. Love to hear the audience slow dance and sing along with this one.

FORGET HIM – a fan favourite and such a beautiful song to sing, sitting on a stool with a single spotlight. Pure magic.

My websites are:- www.colinpaulandthepersuders.co.uk

www.colinpaul.com
email colinpaul1@hotmail.com
Tribute albums recorded....
Colin Paul and The Persuaders
In Thoughts of Billy Fury
Colin Paul – King For Tonight
Colin Paul – In Danger
All are available on iTunes/amazon and websites.

Colin with Billy's Mother, Jean Wycherley

Albert Wycherley onstage with Colin Paul

15: CORA VANAMAN

I have had the pleasure of participating in three different versions of The Billy Fury Show, each with different experiences and at different points in my life.

The first show I took part in was the Nottingham Arts Theatre Production in 2010. I was 14 and looking for new performance opportunities to be part of. My parents found an advertisement in a local newspaper for an audition for this show and we were intrigued. I knew nothing about Billy Fury at this point and I knew no one involved in the production. So I prepared myself for the audition by learning about Billy Fury, basic facts about his life; where he was born, his career, his family and I listened to his songs. This proved to be valuable as the director of the show, Maggie Andrew, sat each person down in the audition to ask what they knew about Billy Fury, as it turned out I was the only one who had done some initial research.

Once making it through the audition, we were each given several of Billy Fury's songs to choreograph to. This was an incredible opportunity for a young aspiring performer; even from a young age I had always choreographed to music and this was my first opportunity to choreograph for a stage show. It was a great system, all the performers involved were allocated songs to choreograph and we were also placed in each other's routines. However it was not without its challenges, I remember we didn't have one rehearsal with the entire cast present, not even the dress rehearsal!

Although this was 10 years ago (as I am writing in 2020) I still remember how much fun I had in this production and the friends I made who are still friends of mine to this day, I will always be grateful for this opportunity which led onto other great opportunities.

After the Arts Theatre production of The Billy Fury Show I never expected to be involved in another version of the same show. So when I learnt that Michael was producing another show to take place at the Mansfield Palace Theatre, in 2011, and that my local dance school had been invited to perform in it I was thrilled for the opportunity to be part of the show a second time. In a similar fashion to the Arts Theatre production, our dance school was allocated some Billy Fury songs to choreograph to. A group of us each choreographed a routine and we performed together in a routine that our dance teacher designed.

We also were given a song to sing for the section about Billy's death, as a group we were to sing Psalm 23 after performing our routines. I was excited to sing this beautiful Psalm however, on the day of the performance my friends felt they didn't know it well enough to feel confident singing in front of an audience. Therefore, I was left alone to sing the Psalm on stage immediately after performing our routines. I was exhausted and terrified, but determined to not let everyone down.

This brings us onto my third and final experience with The Billy Fury Show. In 2015, Michael messaged me asking if I would be interested in directing and choreographing an entire show to be performed in London. It was the day after I had finished a foundation course at Mountview Academy of Theatre Arts, the timing was perfect. I spent the next year planning, researching and choreographing this show. By this point I knew all the songs incredibly well, I knew all about Billy Fury's history and I knew how the show ran as I had performed in two myself. For this production, Michael decided he wanted to use professional dancers, he organised an audition at the Italia Conti Academy of Theatre Arts and I organised an audition at Husky Studios in London. We then began the process of casting our show, we chose a great cast of professional dancers and an actor for the narration.

As this production was different from all the productions we've done before, I wanted to create a narrative that would link the entire show together. All of the individual routines had a story throughout as we follow Ronald Wycherley in his transformation into Billy Fury. We also gave the narrator more of a character and altered the script to indicate that he was Ron's friend telling the audience about his own friend. We still maintained the facts about Billy Fury's life from the original script. I decided to include two male dancers, one to portray Ronald in the early years of his career. The other one to play Billy at the height of his success but being gradually overshadowed by serious illness.

I persuaded Michael to include an assistant director and enlisted the help of Craig Canning who was a huge source of technical help and support to me. The whole process was a big challenge, I had never choreographed on this scale alongside directing, adjusting the script, designing the costumes and lighting and more but it is still one of the most fulfilling experiences and enjoyable productions I've ever been a part of.

Each of the Billy Fury productions I've been involved with has been completely different and all have left me with memories I will carry forever and am grateful for. Michael Parkinson created a show which has honoured Billy Fury's memory in such a wonderful way and brought it to so many people. I am glad to have been a part of it.

Cora and Craig at an early planning meeting with me

Cora's professional publicity picture

Some acting at one of the auditions

Craig and Cora doing research in preparation for the show July

16: DANIEL HEENEY

Hi Michael and thank you for your invitation to include some of my personal background into this story. To be honest I would have absolutely no idea how to write down my history of days on the holiday camps and cruises which although interesting are not really Billy related. So I have kept it short and sweet.

Billy Fury fans are the best and I count myself lucky to have discovered his music and be part of the story. Billy's music has brought together some of the nicest people I have ever met and provided me with so many lovely memories. When I go out I will often be found wearing a jacket with the words 'Billy Fury the legend lives on' or one of my many T shirts and badges with Billy's picture. The usual response is, 'Oh we loved Billy's music' or for those not aware they say 'What was his hit?' I then educate them into how great I think Billy was, giving them statistics, like, he holds the record for the most weeks in the UK singles chart without getting to number one. I mention his songs, films and that the Beatles auditioned to be his backing band etcetera.

I started to listen to Billy Fury back in the 90's, thanks to hearing my Mum's old records and admired the whole Billy sound and the fact he wrote his own songs. It was thanks to social media (Harry Whitehouse-Billyfury.com) I started to attend events and meet the Billy fans. I was also lucky enough to be asked to DJ at various events at the time turning up in my 'Billy Van', which was a van covered with pictures of Billy because, at that time, I was a mobile DJ and children's entertainer. I did the music at Sunnyside in Northampton, an event commemorating Billy's last live show, at a theatre in Newark before the screening of 'Play it Cool' and once for, Billy mega fan and friend I dearly miss, Pat Young, which was for a local charity.

Over the years I managed to convince our local pub (now gone) to have a Billy Fury wall, a wall they covered with music and pictures of Billy. We made a carnival float dedicated to Billy whilst I worked as entertainments manager at Central Beach and it was entered into Leysdown Carnival at Saddlebrook Holiday Park in Kent. I helped with the unveiling of the Billy mural at Billy

Fury Way in London, this was attended by Billy's Mum. I also attended the unveiling of the Blue Plaque at St Johns Wood and the unveiling of the statue in Liverpool. I have supported any Billy Fury tribute or show that I could and at these events and many more I have met hundreds of fellow Billy fans and had some of the greatest nights of my life. I was an extra in the Joe Meek film 'Telstar' and attended the premier.

I know I may not be the greatest magician, I may not be the greatest singer, I may not be the greatest entertainer. What I am is someone who appreciates the hard work of any dedicated Billy fan and tribute acts out there and I will never stop spreading the news of Billy, its up to us fans to keep his legacy going. I often attend Rock n Roll nights with my Teddy-boy drape or Billy Fury shirts on and sometimes with my puppet monkey 'Malcolm'. (also a big Billy fan) and it's all thanks to one of the greatest British Rock n Roll singers we ever had – Billy Fury.

Daniel with Chris Eley (centre) and Colin Paul

The Billy Van

Daniel in full flow

Dan, in his Tommy Cooper role, 'just like that'

With puppet Malcolm who, according to Daniel, is also a Billy Fan

With Vince Eager and Tornados drummer, Clem Cattini

Daniel Heeney with Danny Rivers

With Billy's mum Jean Wycherley

17: JOAN PARKINSON

One of the first television shows that I enjoyed watching was 'Boy Meets Girls', I liked Billy Fury and Marty Wilde best. I left school at fifteen and worked as a cutter in the textile trade and had to get the bus from Broxtowe where I lived to Nottingham. I then had to walk to the factory which was situated at Broad Marsh, about half a mile away. On one of the streets there was a paper shop and I bought a magazine because I recognised pictures from 'Boy meets Girls'. There were stories about Billy Fury, he became my favourite singer so I started to buy his records. The first one was 'Maybe Tomorrow' with 'Gonna Type a Letter' on the other side. I bought more records and even managed to buy his first Album called 'The Sound of Fury'.

I started to buy the 'New Musical Express' each week and noticed that Billy and Marty were going to perform in a show at Derby in October 1962. My friend Kath wanted to go with me so we both got permission from our parents and bought tickets in advance. On Friday 26 October we set off from Mount Street bus station and were both excited as we travelled to Derby. We found the theatre and got in the long queue, we gradually shuffled forward, entered the theatre and were shown to our seats near the front.

They were selling programmes for two shillings each, very expensive, but I bought one. I am looking at it now so that I can write who was on. Al Paige was the compere, first was instrumental group, Peter Jay and the Jaywalkers, then singers Jimmy Justice, Mark Wynter, Marty Wilde, Mike Sarne, Karl Denver Trio and Billy Fury with his backing group The Tornados. Kath and I loved the show, it was great to see and hear people in real life who we had previously only seen on the screen. At the end of the show we went straight to the bus station as it was getting late. We got the bus back to Nottingham and another one home and arrived, tired but happy after a memorable outing.

The family had a radiogram, a large piece of furniture with radio and gramophone combined. There was then a conflict because mum and dad wanted to play their Richard Tauber and Mario Lanza records and my sister her Pat Boone ones.

I wanted to buy a portable record player and saw one in the large Co-op shop in Nottingham but it was 15 guineas, that is 15 pounds 15 shillings. I asked my mother if I could give her some money each week which she could save for me until I had enough. Mum suggested that I speak to the Co-op insurance man who came to the house every month to collect her insurance money. I had to speak to the insurance man myself and he gave me a card on which he wrote the amount of money that I gave him each month. I can't remember how much I gave him a month but after some time he told me that I had enough to buy the record player. He gave me some paperwork for me to take to the Co-op store which would enable me to get the player, he even gave me some discount because I had saved the money so quickly.

One afternoon I left work a bit early and walked up to the Co-op store to collect the record player which was packed in a box, they put some string round it because I told them that I had to take it home on the bus. When I went out of the store I noticed that it had got very foggy but walked to the number 32 bus terminus and was pleased that my bus was there. Many people were waiting but an inspector was stopping everyone getting on. After some time he told us that the bus could not go because the fog was so bad, everyone started walking and I had my parcel to carry with the string cutting into my hands. The distance was three and a half miles to our house in Broxtowe and the fog was so thick that at times I could not even see where to walk, on one occasion I found myself in the middle of the road with a car creeping towards me. When I got home my mother was very relieved to see me, she knew about me collecting the record player but did not know about me having to walk home. I have found out that the date was 5 December 1962. The fog was described as a 'pea souper'.

The player was battery operated, I sometimes played records in my bedroom but the following spring and summer my friend Kath and I used to take it out to fields at nearby Bulwell to play our records. Kath liked Elvis Presley so we listened to Elvis and Billy Fury as we enjoyed the picnic food we took with us.

I got married to Michael Parkinson in May 1970 and we went to live at Keyworth in South Nottinghamshire. He told me that he had seen Billy Fury free of charge when he was performing at the BBC Playhouse theatre in London. About a year later we saw a notice fixed to a post on the edge of a field which we passed every day on our way to work. It was at Ruddington, a tiny village about five miles south of Nottingham and the notice advertised that Billy Fury would be performing there in two weeks time. We were doubtful that it could be the real Billy Fury but saw an advertisement in a local newspaper that confirmed it.

No tickets would be issued, it was just turn up on the evening.

Each time we passed the field we noticed signs of activity, the gateway was enlarged and they put signs out showing where cars could be parked. A couple of days before the event a large canvas marquee was erected. I was excited that I was going to see Billy Fury so close to where we lived. The great day arrived and we made sure that we got there very early to get a good position, it was good that we did. The marquee was not very big and the stage was just a farm cart, there were not many seats but we sat right at the front.

The event was organised by the local Young Farmer's Group. I can't remember a live backing group but there was backing music of some sort. The important thing was that Billy walked up steps at the side and stepped on to the farm cart. He sang a lot more songs than he did when I had seen him at Derby. He was so natural and I was in ecstasy, it was wonderful to be so close to my idol. At the end of the performance Billy stood on the grass and talked to people in a really friendly manner. I remember standing next to him and noticed that he was much taller than me, he was lovely. Some years later Michael and I met Tony Sherwood the theatrical agent who told us that he had organised Billy's appearance at that event and that Billy had agreed to perform at Ruddington because it was for the Young Farmer's Union, a cause that he was interested in.

In 1979 I saw newspaper stories that he was making a comeback and I saw a television interview which included him singing 'Devil or Angel'. Soon afterwards, in December 1982 I was watching television with Marty Wilde on 'This is Your Life'. Towards the end of the show Billy Fury was introduced and I was upset that he looked so poorly. On Friday 28 January 1983 I heard the devastating news on radio that Billy was dead. I felt that I knew him personally because of seeing him perform and so often listening to his records. The funeral was at St John's Wood Church on 4 February and I wept as it was reported on television.

Early in 1995 I was listening to the Brian Matthew BBC Radio show and heard him say something about a Billy Fury musical being performed in Liverpool but did not catch the details. I wrote to Brian asking him about it. To my surprise he sent me a 'Sounds of the Sixties T Shirt' and full details of the show. It was to be performed from 28 June to 12 August 1995 at the Liverpool Playhouse Theatre. I persuaded Michael to take me, my mother and younger sister Karen, so we booked tickets well in advance to get prime position seats for a 5pm Saturday night performance. We could not afford to stay overnight so set off from Nottingham early in the morning, we arrived at Liverpool and parked near the docks overlooking the Mersey. We sat out on a seat and ate our sandwiches and enjoyed a drink from our flasks. We then went round the 'Beatles Experience' because Karen loved the Beatles and then visited a little exhibition near the docks.

We noticed that they were doing boat trips round the docks so went on a boat. We got back in the car and went to the car park near to the Liverpool Playhouse so parked up well before the show. We were close to the famous 'Cavern' where The Beatles and Cilla Black had performed so visited that place. It was then time to get changed into our posh clothes and went into the theatre which was sold out. The show was absolutely fabulous, Danny McCall played the role of Billy Fury, his acting and singing were great. I bought a programme. We all really enjoyed the show and I thought that Danny McCall did the best impersonation of Billy Fury that I have ever seen. When the show finished Michael bought me a T shirt and Karen bought me a Billy Fury mug before we set off back to Nottingham. It was a day out that I will never forget.

A few years later, in 2003, I was listening to 'Sounds of the Sixties' and Brian Mathew said that a statue of Billy Fury was to be erected in the Liverpool dockland area so when it was done I decided that I wanted to see it. Some time later the Daily Mail offered a cheap rail ticket deal so I persuaded Michael to book two tickets for us to visit Liverpool on a midweek day. We went on the train to Liverpool Lime Street and went on a bus to the docks. I asked a lady who was sitting in the bus shelter which number bus was going to the terminal for the ferry across the Mersey. As we chatted I found out that she used to live near Ronnie before he was famous as Billy Fury and that he used to sing in the local pub at Dingle. We got off the bus and found the statue which I thought was a really good likeness of him.

We then went on the ferry which goes from Liverpool docks to Birkenhead and Seacombe and were allowed to stay on the ferry or we would have had to wait an hour for the next boat back. It was my ambition to do this because of the Gerry and the Pacemakers song 'Ferry across the Mersey'. We went back on the bus from the docks and got the train back to Nottingham. I love Liverpool and the Billy Fury connection so really enjoyed our day out.

Four years later, in 2007, I found out that the bronze statue which was sculptured by fellow Liverpudlian Tom Murphy was moved and placed near the Albert Dock where young Ronnie had worked on a tugboat. That was a perfect excuse to ask Michael to take me to Liverpool again so in 2009 we visited Liverpool and saw the statue in the new position at the dockside.

In 2009 Michael was writing the script for a Billy Fury Dance show and Chris

Eley of the Sound of Fury Fan Club started to send CDs which we listened to whilst deciding what songs to include in the show. I listened to many Billy songs that I had not heard before and I really enjoyed the experience. One morning we discovered a song that we both loved, it was called 'In My Room', we put it on repeat play and listened to it about six times, it was a must for the show. The CDs arrived spaced out over a period of time so over about six weeks we had the difficult task of what to include and what to leave out. We worked together for ages on the project and Michael was continually asking my opinion about many things. I started to think that I knew Billy because of all the research and work we did.

The show was performed at the Nottingham Arts Theatre for two nights in July 2010, it was a hectic time for us both. I had to prepare for Chris and Linda who stayed for a couple of nights with us. I loved the show, it was great listening to all the songs that we had selected and watching the girls dancing to them. The highlight was that Billy's mother Jean came to the show and I was delighted to meet her. To our amazement Chris had organised pictures to be presented to Jean, us and Mags Cummings who had brought Jean all the way from Liverpool. In addition I won a framed picture of Billy Fury that Chris Eley had donated as a raffle prize. That sell out show was a fantastic success and when it was all over Chris, Linda Michael and I sat outside our house till the small hours of the morning enjoying drinks and food.

We put the show on again at Lytham St Annes (near Blackpool) on Sunday 2 October 2011 and stayed in a plush room at the Clifton Arms Hotel for four days. I really enjoyed it although we were busy working on the show.

The next one was at the Mansfield Palace Theatre on Saturday 8 October, only six days later, and I had an unfortunate experience. On the morning of the show Michael drove round to the back of the theatre and was able to park the car there for the whole day. When the performers and dance captains arrived they were all preparing for the technical rehearsal and I was going backwards and forwards to the car taking various things in to the theatre. The staff had allocated a table to me, near the stage, for raffle prizes and ticket selling. I had carried things through the stage door across the backstage area and down some steps to put near the table. I had to avoid everyone who was doing the rehearsal on stage. I was happily singing along, as a Billy Fury song was being played, and setting the raffle prizes out, when the safety curtain came down trapping me on my own in the auditorium. The lights were on so I went to the door at the back but it was locked, I tried shouting but no one responded. I found a small door that I knew went to the backstage area, it was locked so I banged on it loudly. After about five minutes a lady opened the door and escorted me through a kitchen area that was being used as an additional dressing room and to the backstage area. I told the technical man about my predicament, he told me they were just testing the safety curtain and opened it for me. Michael and I always have a laugh when the safety curtain comes down in a theatre but I was not laughing at the time. The show was a great success and we donated £520.70 to Jessies Fund from the Lytham and Mansfield shows.

The next show was at the Floral Pavilion, New Brighton on Sunday 1 April 2012. The theatre is situated on the opposite side of the Mersey to Liverpool docks where young Ronald Wycherley had worked before finding fame as Billy Fury. We booked into a hotel close to the theatre on the Tuesday prior to the show. One day we went on the bus to Liverpool so looked at the statue again before looking around the Museum of Liverpool where Billy Fury features in the section called Wondrous Place. We then went back into the City and looked around the shopping centre which is called 'Liverpool One'. We got the bus back to New Brighton after another enjoyable trip to one of my favourite places.

Michael had invited Billy's mother to the show but she replied that she would be in Germany so would not be able to accept. Four days before the show Michael had a meeting with technical staff at the theatre so I went with him and sat in the coffee bar area and enjoyed a peaceful afternoon looking out over the Mersey and watching the boats. We went to the theatre early on the day of the show and a full dress rehearsal took place in the afternoon. I was in the foyer area doing my usual job of setting out raffle prizes when a man from the theatre told me that Jean Wycherley (Billy's mother) was in a car outside, asking if she could come to the show. I told him to see Michael who went out to give Jean a ticket, he came back and told me that he had arranged for her to speak to the audience at the end of the show and that she would be sitting in the seat that Michael was saving for himself next to me.

After the dress rehearsal we went back to the hotel and got changed ready for the evening show. When we went back to the theatre it became hectic because loads of people wanted to buy raffle tickets though the theatre staff sold programmes. I was last in the theatre for the start of the show and Jean was in position next to me when I took my seat.

She kept telling me how much she was enjoying the show and at the end spoke to the audience and suggested an encore of 'Halfway to Paradise'. To my surprise Jean grabbed the microphone and accompanied the recorded voice of her son.

134

When it was finished she got a standing ovation with thunderous applause, I felt honoured to be standing next to her.

In 2015 Michael and I were invited by Lisa Voice (Billy's partner) to attend a prestigious show in London. It was to be at the Grand Connaught Rooms on Great Queen Street, some Billy Fury items were to be included in a 'Celebrity Auction' and there was to be a dinner and star studded show. Chris Eley and Linda were also invited and we were told that we would be sharing a table with them. There was a problem though, the tickets that we were told were in the post did not arrive before we left from Nottingham on the morning of the event. Michael and Chris had been in constant telephone contact and Chris understood that the tickets for all four of us had been sent to his address in Chichester. As they would not be leaving home until late morning he assumed that they would arrive before they left home. We were told that the dress code would be 'Cocktail/Suit attire' so took a change of clothes with us. During the afternoon Chris phoned to say that the tickets had not arrived but that they would be at the Connaught reception for us. They were not there when we arrived at the Connaught Rooms at 6:30pm for the 7:30 start. The staff told us not to worry so we got changed and Chris and Linda arrived, he had received a telephone message that Lisa was bringing our tickets in so no need to worry. As we waited I talked to a couple who were in the same predicament as us. They had met one of the stars, Dorothy Moore, (Misty Blue) in America and she had invited them to the event but their tickets were not at reception.

The staff told us to go up to the room and wait which we eventually did. Chris had brought a large framed picture of Billy Fury with the Tornados which he planned to donate to the auction but was told that it was not registered so they refused his offer. Michael and Chris did a deal so Michael bought the picture which has pride of place in our hallway.

We felt like uninvited guests and Michael kept joking that, 'our fall back position is the chippy at St Pancras'. The start of the show was delayed, as we waited, Bill Wyman (Rolling Stones) and his wife came in and stood near us. We chatted to him and he said how much he liked Billy Fury and how sad it was that he died so young. Michael told them about our ticket problem. Bill and his wife found it hilarious that our 'fall back position was the St Pancras chippy'.

Eventually a waiter came to us and asked us to sit at a round table set for ten people, by then it was nearly an hour past the starting time and there were still plenty of empty seats. I spotted the Dorothy Moore couple sitting up in the balcony which was for people who had booked entertainment only so I told

Michael that I felt sorry for them and I went up some stairs to the balcony. They were very upset that Dorothy had not organised tickets as she had promised to do in America. I acted quite out of character and told them to come and sit with us. They went down stairs with me and joined us at the table. There was then an announcement that everyone should start the wine so we all had a drink or two or three. I loved it, because there were many stars that I recognised, one of them who came and talked to us was Robbie from Eastenders. After a while the head waiter came and asked us to move to another table but not to take any wine with us. So, we, and the couple that I had invited, moved to the table that he indicated and had to start the unopened wine there. Some of us had rather a lot of wine but not Michael because he had to drive when we got off the train home. They then started the auction and the couple that I had invited bought a voucher for four people at an expensive restaurant, I think they paid £100 for it.

The waiters started to serve the meal which was lovely and after a while Lisa arrived with our tickets but nobody wanted to look at them. They started the entertainment as the meal was being served. It was billed as David Gest's (I've Had) The Time of My Life Tour. There was Bill Medley, Sheila Ferguson, Deniece Williams, Billy Paul, The Tymes, Freda Payne, Cece Peniston, Dorothy Moore, Barbara Weathers and a full backing orchestra. At one point in the evening Dorothy Moore came to our table and chatted with the couple that I had invited. Lisa came over and spoke to us very pleasantly, I don't think that anyone mentioned the ticket fiasco but I had drunk enough wine not to care. It was all running very late so Michael and I had to drag ourselves away because we were booked on the latest train back to Nottingham. Chris and Linda were able to stay until the end because they were booked into a hotel overnight. We went from the sumptuous surrounding of the Connaught Rooms and got the number 91 bus to St Pancras arriving home in the early hours of the morning after a memorable day.

The next show was a very different experience. It was performed at the Shaw Theatre in London from 14 to 23 of April 2016 with professional dancers. We had to find somewhere to stay for two weeks in central London and eventually found the Youth Hostel Association place at St Pancras. This is not restricted to young people, as the name suggests, so we booked in for two weeks. Our room was on the top floor which we thought would be quiet but I was constantly woken up by emergency sirens and noise from the road below. We combined going to all the thirteen performances of the show and went to various places around London on business or pleasure. The Shaw Theatre is in the Pullman St

Pancras hotel and was very plush so again I enjoyed repeatedly listening to the Billy Fury tracks and watching the cast perform.

The day of the last shows was traumatic for both of us because we had arranged to go home on the train that night after the second performance of the day finished. We had to book out of the hostel after breakfast on the Saturday morning, and fortunately the staff of the Shaw Theatre arranged to store our cases for us. That bit was easy because after we had taken the cases across we could relax until the afternoon performance started. I enjoyed the matinee performance and again we had time to relax before the evening performance began but at the end of that performance things were hectic. Michael, Cora, Craig and the performers had to handle what they call the 'get out'. That means clearing everyone connected with the show and all their possessions out of the theatre and saying goodbye to people.

We managed that all right but the difficult bit for Michael and I was that Cora and Craig could not manage to take all the costumes and props to their lodgings with them so we had to take them with us on the train. There were many boxes of stuff plus a portable typewriter, my portable record player and our cases. The theatre staff were great, because four of them walked with us from the theatre to St Pancras station with the six of us carrying things between us. The four helpers waited with us until the train was ready to board and the station staff allowed them to go through the ticket barriers to get all our stuff on to the train.

That left Michael and I on the train with all the things around us. Fortunately the late night train was not too busy so the only problem was getting everything off when it stopped at East Midlands Parkway station. As the train approached our destination we got all our belongings near the door, When the train stopped we had a stroke of good luck because the platform staff knew Michael well. They opened a gate that allowed us to get out of the station easily and whilst Michael brought the car round they brought all the belongings round with me and even helped to put it in the car.

Over the next few weeks I washed all the stage clothes and packed them in boxes that we stored in our loft. They remained there until Michael donated them to the Nottingham Arts Theatre. I believe that my story is typical of the many unsung heroes who support theatrical events and dance schools.

Front of the programme for the show at Derby

THE
Mammoth Star Show
OF 1962

presented by LARRY PARNES   ★★★★★★★★★★★★★★★★★★★★★★★

AL PAIGE
YOUR HOST AND COMPERE

PETER JAY and the JAYWALKERS
DYNAMIC INSTRUMENTAL GROUP

JIMMY JUSTICE
HIT RECORDING STAR

MARK WYNTER
INTERNATIONAL TEENAGE STAR

MARTY WILDE
BRITAIN'S VERSATILE YOUNG ENTERTAINER

MIKE SARNE
"COME OUTSIDE"

JOE BROWN and the BRUVVERS
BRITAIN'S BRIGHTEST STARS

THE KARL DENVER TRIO
STARS OF THE HIT PARADE

Star of TV, Stage, Radio, Films and Records

BILLY FURY
AND HIS TORNADOS

God Save the Queen

This programme is subject to alteration at the discretion of the management

| Tour Management and Administration | MARK FORSTER |
| Stage Manager | GORDON MARSHALL |

In accordance with the requirements of the local authorities, where applicable: 1. The Public may leave at the end of the performance by all exit and entrance doors, and such doors must at that time be open. 2. All gangways, passages and staircases must be kept entirely free from chairs or obstruction. 3. The safety curtain must be lowered and raised once, immediately before the commencement of each performance, so as to ensure its being in proper working order. No smoking permitted to take place on the stage except as part of the performance or entertainment.

List of performers at the first show that I attended

139

Programme for a great show at Liverpool

The front of the programme for the show at the Connaught Rooms, London

My old record player was used in the show at the Shaw Theatre 2016 show

I carried this home because of the 'pea souper' on 5 December 1962

Rolling Stone, Bill Wyman and his wife thought it was hilarious that our fall back position was the chippy at St Pancras

18: MAGS CUMMINGS

I first saw Billy Fury at the Manchester Hippodrome in 1959 when I was fifteen years old and was completely hooked by his amazing stage performance and charisma. I learned that a show called Wham, produced by Jack Good, was about to be televised from the ABC studios in Didsbury Manchester. I cycled there with a friend every other week and was fortunate to meet many of the stars featured in the show. Marty Wilde, Joe Brown, Michael Cox and Jess Conrad were some that I met and of course, Billy.

We went early to catch rehearsals when many of the guys would come outside for a breath of air. The first time I spoke to him was when he came out and asked whether there was a shop nearby that sold cigarettes. I told him there was one along the road, over a bridge and further on and offered to show him where. A few girls, that we had befriended, came along too, I linked arms with him and asked what he was doing after Wham. He said that he had a summer season in Great Yarmouth coming. We just chatted about general things but he seemed very shy and nervous.

I saw him in Manchester again in a show and gave him a card on stage and he sat me down and sang Halfway to Paradise to me. The girls in the audience were going wild with envy. My next personal encounter was in Buxton, we met him before the show and had photos with him. His birthday was approaching and a friend and I had made him a cake and huge card which I handed to him on stage during the show. He sang 'A Thousand Stars' to me, much to my delight. Later, the gate he wanted to go through with the car, was locked and Hal Carter, his road manager went to get help. I decided to try and slide under the gate and succeeded. I ran up to the car and he recognised me, saying, 'you gave me the cake didn't you? Tell you what, come here'. I leaned into the open car window and he gave me a very long kiss, my first ever. Moving on, I met Billy on many more occasions becoming friends.

Sometimes he would ask me and a couple of friends to stay with him and talk whilst he was signing autographs before shows as he was nervous. I became good friends with Wendy White, one of his fan club secretaries, so got even more access to him. I have many stories to tell including the time he gave a friend and me a lift to our caravan in his car when he saw us swaying along the promenade in Great Yarmouth after drinking too much. He warned us to stay inside for the rest of the night. He was 22 years old and sounded like our dad, he was so caring.

During this period a friend and I went to Billy's parents house in Mossley Hill and met Albie, his brother who took us for a spin in his new car. It started to rain and his mum asked us in and gave us sandwiches, cakes and tea. She sent his dad into the loft to bring down lots of things Billy had been given by fans, including my huge birthday cards.

The cake, that I had given him at Buxton, was in the display cabinet!

On another occasion Billy came over from the waiting room, on the opposite side of the track, to chat to my friend and I whilst we were waiting for a train home after a show in Stoke. He told us he had just recorded Jealousy and we must have talked for about 15 minutes. He gave each of us a kiss and waved until the train disappeared from sight.

I got married and didn't see Billy again as we had a little boy and my husband John was abroad working a lot so I couldn't get to any of his shows. When Billy tragically died I was absolutely devastated.

I always wished to meet his mum again and my wish was granted the day before the official statue unveiling at the Museum of Life in Liverpool. (The statue was later moved to the Albert Dock). It was a press day, when a mutual friend and Billy tribute singer, Ray Shenton, introduced me to Jean and Albie and we became very close friends.

I was also introduced to Billy Fury weekends, organised by Blackpool Holidays, run by Diane Wardle and her Mum Mrs Roth. I took Jean to Mill Hill gatherings organised by the Sound of Fury fan club on a few occasions. We then started Liverpool meetings with 'Billy Fury In Thoughts of You' fan club, I built and ran the club website. Jenny Warwick, who had bought Billy's farm in Wales, was the club secretary.

My husband John and I took Jean to see a wonderful dance show in Nottingham, produced by Michael Parkinson. The youngsters taking part interpreted Billy songs into dance and it was truly magical. Jean thoroughly enjoyed it and it was well worth the trip. The journey started from Poynton, Cheshire, where we lived, Liverpool to collect Jean, on to Nottingham and the return journey made a total of over 300 miles.

During the latter years sadly Albie passed away. I had got to know him very well as we had spoken a lot about the fan club website on the telephone. In addition I saw him in Blackpool and Liverpool and had visited him at home with friends and Jean.

A friend and I often visited Jean, both in hospital and at home until she too passed away at the grand age of 96. I have so many wonderful memories and feel very blessed to have been friends with Billy and his family.

Mags with Billy many years ago

Mags with her friend outside Billy's rental house at Great Yarmouth in 1962

Billy and Mags at the Floral Hall Southport in the early 60s, she must have said something to make him laugh.

Mags with Jean Wycherley at a Billy Fury weekend

19: MALCOLM SPEARING

I was born in 1954 at Seacombe in Wallasey, which is on the opposite bank of the Mersey from Liverpool Docks, but have always been proud of my Liverpool connections and like to regard myself as a 'Scouser'. However, to some Liverpudlians I am known as a 'Plastic Scouser' because I live across the Mersey from the Liver Building. It is a similar situation to the definition of Cockneys in London where anyone born within the sound of the bells from St Mary Le Bow Church can regard themselves as a Cockney. I believe that the definition of a 'Scouser' should be anyone living within earshot of the clock on the Royal Liver Building. But there are no bells inside the clock towers. It made no sound at all until 1953 when a chiming mechanism was installed in memory of Royal Liver staff killed during both world wars. The chimes are made using piano wires hit by hammers, the sound is amplified using a microphone, amplifier and speaker.

I now live at New Brighton which is directly across the Mersey from Liverpool Docks where the famous statue of Billy Fury is situated. I became aware of Billy Fury when I was about 7, I had a sister who was seven years older than me who was into the Mersey scene of the Beatles, Gerry Marsden, Billy Fury and others. So the music was all around me at home. I developed a particular interest in the songs of Billy Fury and can remember liking 'Halfway to Paradise', 'Jealousy' and later 'It's only Make Believe'.

I had the privilege, no honour, to meet Billy's mum, Jean Wycherley, on two occasions. The first was at the Nottingham Art's Theatre where I had gone to attend Michael Parkinson's Billy Fury Dance Show on 10 July 2010. She stepped out of the car outside the theatre and I knew then she was something special. What a lovely lady she was, and throughout the performance I took the opportunity to look across at her. You could tell she was proud of her son, of what he had achieved, and enjoyed the photos and songs. I spoke to her after the performance and she told me how much she had enjoyed the young dancers performing to Billy's songs. There was a song in that show that I had never heard before, it was called 'In My Room' and I loved it'.

The second occasion I met her was in my home town of New Brighton, Wirral, at the 'The Floral Pavilion Theatre' which also happens to be where I got married. It was another Michael Parkinson Dance Show performed on 1 April 2012. Then again I sat near her and was stunned by the elegance of this lady, she watched the show but surprised us by making a speech at the end. She asked the dancers to do an encore of 'Halfway to Paradise' and sang along as the Billy Fury recording was played. This put me to no doubt to where he got his singing voice. The audience gave her a standing ovation which she accepted gracefully. Even at the grand age of ninety-one she still had it! I am so glad I was able to meet her and I will treasure those moments I had with her.

I am proud of my connection with Liverpool and one local man who helped young Ronald Wycherley on his way was Percy Phillips who set up his own revolutionary sound recording studio at 38 Kensington in Liverpool.

Percy was born in 1896 at Warrington, he was a soldier in the first world war but was injured before returning home in 1914. He started selling cycles and motorcycles in a little shop in Brunswick Street in the Kensington Fields area of Liverpool and in 1925 he opened a shop in the front room of his family's three-storey Georgian terraced house. He called it 'Phillips' Battery Charging Depot' and installed large accumulators in the cellar. He continued to run the business throughout the second world war but in the1950s there was a decline in demand for batteries so he started selling household electrical goods and progressed into selling records and record players.

Sales of American country and western and big band records soared, helped by the large contingent of American forces stationed at RAF Burtonwood Air Base, situated on the Liverpool side of Warrington. It was the largest military airbase in the UK during world war two but the RAF passed the base over to the Americans in 1942. There were over eighteen thousand United States servicemen and women stationed there and the shop benefitted from their custom.

Phillips had established useful contacts at Burtonwood which enabled him to set up trade deals with the Americans. Around 1945 Percy planned to set up a sound recording system and obtained information from his son, Frank, who was attending a course on that subject at EMI Electronics in London. Percy bought a 1/4 inch tape recorder, an MSS (Marguerite Sound Studios) disc cutting machine, an amplifier, a 4-track mixer, three microphones, one Reslo, HMV ribbon microphone, (this allowed two vocalists to sing simultaneously on either side), and four special headphone sets at a cost of £400.

He set up the equipment in the small room between the shop and the back kitchen. He put a piano and an overturned tin bath in the cellar as a reverb chamber, with a speaker and microphone linked to the studio above. The recordings would normally be on tape, and then transferred to disc, although the tape was recorded over again for each session. Because of trams, trucks, and horses passing the premises, Phillips hung heavy blankets over the studio door and a rear window to minimise noise intrusion. His first recording was of himself singing 'Bonnie Marie of Argyle', unaccompanied, and a few days later he recorded 'Unchained Melody', with local dance band singer Betty Roy. The first disc he cut in the studio was on 7 August 1955, with his eight-year-old daughter, Carol, singing, 'Mr Sandman'. All the discs had 'Play with a light-weight pick-up' on the label, as this would increase the life of the disc, before it eventually wore out. (I am indebted to the internet for some of this information MS).

Percy renamed his shop 'Phillips Sound Recording Services' and young Ronald Wycherley was one of the first budding stars to get a demonstration disc made there. From this Ron paid for the famous tape that he sent to Larry Parnes in 1958. Other unknown people, at the time, who later used the recording facilities were John Lennon, Paul McCartney, George Harrison, Ken Dodd and Marty Wilde. I went to 38 Piccadilly in December 2020 to take pictures that are included in this book and was disappointed that there was no plaque mentioning Billy Fury. There was a huge plaque featuring 'The Quarrymen' a skiffle group, some of them, went on to become internationally famous as 'The Beatles'. They had recorded a disc called 'That'll Be The Day' in that house.

Phillips business cards included the words 'PF Phillips, 38 Kensington, Liverpool, 7. Television and Battery Service. Gramophone Record Dealer. Professional Tape and Disc Recording Studio.' He cut discs for members of the public, and actors from the Liverpool Playhouse, who often stayed in the first-floor boarding rooms above the studio. Many of the actors asked Phillips to record monologues and poems. These included the actors John Thaw, Richard Briers, and ventriloquist Ray Alan. For the first couple of years, Phillips made music compilation discs for local businesses such as the local ice rink or cinema, men singing songs for loved ones, children playing an instrument, or even a neighbour's dog howling along to piano accompaniment. As the record shop and studio took over the business, he had a brass plate made which he put on the wall just outside the front door. He had labels made for the discs, but changed the design of the disc label every year. Percy Phillips had established his name in the Liverpool Hall of Fame and his place in musical history, he died in 1984.

Bernie Taupin, and Martin Page wrote the words to a song called Billy Fury.

Taupin has been a lyricist to Elton John for more than 50 years and he included the Billy Fury track on his album named 'Tribe', released in 1987. This included Bernie and Elton singing supportive vocals and can be seen on YouTube under the title 'Bernie Taupin & Elton John – Billy Fury'. The description states:- Billy Fury was a Merseyside Rock and Roll legend who died in 1983.

The house where Percy Phillips started his business

A closer look

There is a sign about the Beatles but Ronald Wycherley was one of the first to use the studio

An impressive sign about the Quarrymen who were founded by John Lennon, at the Quarry Bank School in Liverpool before acquiring other members, and becoming internationally famous as 'The Beatles'.

20: Marina Weedon

I come from a large family of ten children, 3 boys and 7 girls, we lived at Acton, Dad was a glass blower at a factory in Potters Bar. As we all got a bit older we had a different taste in music. My sister Rose is six years older than me and she was Elvis, Billy and all those singers who were around then. I heard her playing one of her records, I did not know who it was then, I must have been around 13 or 14, I asked her who the singer was and she said Billy Fury, I think it was 'Maybe Tomorrow' (it was so long ago I can't properly remember). I said he sounds lovely, such a creamy voice and from that day I was in love with Billy. When I left school at 15 I went to work in a factory and started to earn money, so as soon as I could I got my first record player on hire purchase as you did in those days. I then started my collection of Billy's records.

When I was sixteen my sister Rose and I went to see Billy in a show at the Southall Dominion Theatre as my birthday treat. My parents had given me a brand new watch and I wore it for the first time for the show. Whilst Billy was performing I was screaming and jumping up and down with all the other girls and we loved it. At the end of the show we were getting ready to leave so I looked for the time on my watch and to my dismay it was missing. Rose and I searched all around but it was nowhere to be seen. We asked at the theatre office who took our details and said they would let us know if it was handed in. We were very late home because of the delay and I had to tell my Dad that the watch was lost, he was furious and vowed never to buy me another one. I was so sad that I had lost my watch but at least I had got to see Billy so that made me happy.

I soon joined the Billy Fury fan club and they sent me two tickets to see Billy in Yarmouth so again myself and sister Rose met up in London with other fans and boarded a coach which set off for Yarmouth. The journey was fun and we arrived in time to have a look round before the show. Later, on our way to the theatre, we got some chips but they would not allow us into the theatre with them so we hid them in our bag and ate them before the show started. When Billy came on stage I did not scream or jump about, I was more grown up this time, the other girls were screaming but not me. My sister, Rose, was in the Marty Wilde fan club and was given a ticket to meet the performers after a show at the Royal Albert Hall in London. As the fans jostled to get autographs Rose said stop pushing and was surprised that Billy Fury heard her and said yes, stop pushing, you will all have your turn, in a loud but friendly voice.

Over the years I got most, if not all, of Billy's records including 45s, LPs and EPs. The sounds in our home were me with Billy, my brother Dennis with Bob Dylan, Rose with her mixture and my sister Gladys with Cliff Richard.

I got married to Paul in 1969 and went to live at Chiswick, we later had a boy called Stephen, and I continued enjoying Billy's music. Paul and I had problems and were divorced in 1980. Around 1997 Stephen and I went to a little record shop at Chiswick which was run by a guy called Terry (who has since passed away). He sold all the old stuff from the 60s, and as we were chatting Terry gave me some lovely pictures of Billy and told me about the Sound of Fury Fan Club that had just started up. He gave me the telephone number of Chris Eley so I rang him and was soon a member.

Not long after getting details of where Billy's grave was, Stephen, my son, came with me for the first time, we had a lot of trouble getting there but it was worth it. Then I found out about Billy Fury nights at the Ace Cafe, and enjoyed going to them. My ex-husband started going to those nights with me and though we were no longer married we went there on a few occasions. He is a taxi driver and started to take me to Billy's grave at Mill Hill, he would sit on Billy's bench whilst I trimmed the two bushes and tidied the grave. Paul would help with carrying the heavy watering cans for me, then we would drive to the Ace Cafe for lunch. One day when we were at the grave the groundsman's jeep stopped near us and this guy got out and spoke to Paul and then came over to speak to me, it was the lovely Michael Parkinson who had travelled on the train from Nottingham. It was so nice to meet him and we have stayed in touch ever since.

Paul and I continued going to Billy's grave every two to three weeks and then on to the Ace Cafe, it was fun. Times have changed again now, Paul and I are getting older, we are both 74 and I have not seen him for a while but he rings me nearly every week. We have not been to Mill Hill for around three years now, it's a shame, but that's life. Billy Fury is always around my home, he's on my walls, I have so many pictures of him and I can play my Billy music whenever I'm in the mood for his songs. In conclusion I am proud of our son Stephen who works at the West Middlesex University Hospital, London.

My three favourite songs by Billy are:-

I Will
I'm Lost Without You
You're Swell (from the film Play it Cool)

Love to all the fans Marina x

Caption Marina at the grave that she tended

The Blue Plaque outside the apartment where Billy Fury lived at 1 Cavendish Ave, St John's Wood, London NW8 9JE

Marina against the mural at Billy Fury Way

21: MARION CAVE

Marion has given permission for her booklet, Billy Fury Biography, published in 2011, to be included here. Michael Parkinson.

The Early Years

Billy was born Ronald Wycherley in 1940 in Liverpool where he lived with his parents Jean and Albert and brother Albie. Although his childhood was marred by illness he enjoyed caring for animals and birds and often brought home injured strays. Rheumatic fever left Billy with a damaged heart, which affected him all his life. As a teenager he enjoyed writing poems and songs in the hope of a break into showbiz. After brief jobs on the Liverpool tugboats and in a clothes shop, the break came. In October 1958 he auditioned for impresario Larry Parnes at the Essoldo, Birkenhead. Larry was so impressed he named him Billy Fury and put him straight into the show with Marty Wilde and other artistes managed by him. Later in 1958 Billy had his first hit with Maybe Tomorrow, which he wrote himself. Although the package tours in those days were gruelling for someone in perfect health Billy soon learnt to cope. He could captivate an audience completely and send his ever growing band of fans wild. The sexy on stage image was far removed from the shy, caring, animal loving person he really was.

My Meeting with Billy

In 1959, at the age of 7, I was in hospital and so upset I could not go to the concert my Mum had promised to take me to. I had decided that I was a fan after hearing Maybe Tomorrow. So I wrote to Billy via the record company, not really thinking my letter would be read by him. Imagine how I felt when he visited me in hospital and promised tickets for a show when I was better. He kept his promise with a V.I.P day out for me and my Mum and from then on we corresponded and met as often as possible. I considered him a dear friend for the rest of his life. As well as the music, we shared a life-long love of horses, so there was always lots to talk about when we got together. I know that many of Billy's other fans also knew him as a friend. He would always arrange parties and get-to-gethers and always take an interest in what we were up to. He liked to talk to his fans but sometimes he had to escape some, who tried to tear his clothes and go crazy. Such was his stage act!

The Sixties

The Sixties were an exciting time, the music, the clothes and so much to look forward to. Billy had perfected his stage act, the gold lamé suits were still there, but he had toned it down a bit, after raising a few eyebrows. In 1960 he undertook his first Summer Season at Great Yarmouth. The first of many shows he was to do there. Many happy memories and good friendships were to start there. It gave him a chance to perform with people like Carl Denver and the Bachelors, not just the Rock n Roll set. 1961 was a very significant year. As a 21st birthday present Larry Parnes took Billy to the States to meet his idol, Elvis Presley. He met Elvis on his film set, a dream come true and an experience that he never forgot. This was also the year of one of Billy's biggest hits 'Halfway to Paradise'. The song was not written by Billy but by Goffin and King. Nevertheless it suited Billy perfectly and in a way the lyrics summed up his life.

The following year Billy embarked on a new phase in his career, acting. He started filming 'Play it Cool' a cleverly penned story line in which Billy played a popstar who rescues an heiress from a criminal boyfriend. The film also featured many other young singers, some of whom remained life long friends with Billy. Two of them were Bobby Vee and Helen Shapiro. The Michael Winner directed film was a great box office success and gained Billy even more fans. It also gave us another hit 'Twist Kid'. 'Play it Cool' reflected the fun side of the sixties and left most people with a happy feeling. From 1963 to 1966 Billy had his own magazine 'Fury Monthly' which kept everyone up to date with what he was doing. It also kept the fans in touch with one another and was full of great photographs, which of course are still treasured today. Billy even ran an advice column for fans!

His love of horses progressed in 1964 when he bought a racehorse named 'Anselmo'. The horse had already been entered for the Derby and Billy was very excited at the prospect of being in the owner's enclosure. Billy met the Queen and mingled with owners and trainers. A very memorable day especially as Anselmo came fourth in the race.

The whole event gave Larry Parnes the idea to make another film. So in the summer of 1965 work began on Billy's second film 'I've Gotta Horse'. This film, in which Billy played himself, was a true reflection of his personality. It was set in Great Yarmouth during one of Billy's summer seasons there, and of course included Derby Day. There were great performances from Amanda Barrie, Michael Medwin and the very funny Bill Fraser. Billy also had his beloved dogs in the film who also behaved very well. It was all put together so well that it gave the audience an insight into the person Billy really was. Not just a sexy popstar in a gold lamé suit but a very kind gentle person who loved his animals and the countryside. I have special memories of the film as I visited Billy on the set and saw how much everyone enjoyed the making of it. Billy also starred in 'Aladdin' at Oxford in 1965. It was his only pantomime but another unforgettable experience.

Away from showbiz Billy had his house in the country where he could relax and be himself. He loved birdwatching and photography of birds and wildlife. He would spend hours in a bird hide, or even up a tree, to get the picture he wanted. He even produced a book of bird photographs. Billy also took in a lot of injured birds and animals of all kinds. At his house in Surrey, he turned a disused swimming pool into a bird sanctuary. I remember an injured swan he nursed back to health and then taught him to swim again by wading into the water with the bird.

Billy did so much for animals, most of the time out of the public eye. For instance, he went to Cornwall after the Torrey Canyon oil-tanker disaster, to help clean the stricken sea birds. He also went to Norfolk, to administer medication to seals, when a virus affected the babies. Billy also campaigned for the banning of hunting, a fight that still goes on of course. Eventually his battle with huntsmen, invading his land, led to him selling his house in Surrey and buying one in Kent.

In 1968 he bought another racehorse 'First Rate Pirate', not so talented on the course as Anselmo, but Billy always said he was the best horse he had ever ridden. He became more of a pet and later was to inspire Billy to breed horses.

1969 was a bit of a turning point in Billy's life. First of all Larry Parnes stepped down as his manager. I think Larry felt they had gone as far possible. Billy having done package tours, TV and films etcetera. Billy increasingly wanted to do his own thing with his farm. There was also the question of whether he should record other people's songs or record his own material. He did both well so it was an unanswered question. Hal Carter took over as Billy's manager. He had previously worked with Billy as personal assistant, so they knew each other well.

On 31 May 1969 Billy married his fiancé, Judith Hall. Unfortunately for many reasons the marriage did not last.

Looking Back at The Sixties

Billy had 26 chart hits in nine years. He had toured with just about everyone on the pop scene. He had met the great Elvis Presley. His unique rapport with his adoring fans would only get stronger as they grew up together. What now? There was so much he wanted to do, how would he manage his career with his love of animals and the countryside? There was always the worry, amongst friends and family, that he would overdo things. His heart problems were never far away but he was always determined not to let anyone down.

Into the Seventies

Billy decided that Cabaret was the next step, they were more relaxed than package tours which had taken their toll on his health and he could get closer to the audience. He could talk to his fans, most of whom he looked on as friends. Once he got used to this change of venue, it was a great success. The autumn of 1971 brought a bitter blow to all of us, as it became apparent that Billy needed major heart surgery. An operation to repair damaged heart valves meant Christmas in the National Heart hospital in London. It was a very worrying time for all of us. Billy made good progress and received thousands of cards, letters and presents from well wishers. When he arrived home he set about writing to as many of his fans as possible. He could not believe how much people cared. It took him a lot longer to recover than he thought and his planned tour for 1972 had to be cancelled on doctor's orders. Billy was disappointed, feeling he was letting everyone down. So, instead, he did a series of radio shows with Johnnie Walker. The shows proved very popular and helped Billy gradually get back to work.

By August 1972 Billy was back to normal and very excited to be invited to take part in what was to be one of the biggest ever Rock n Roll concerts. It took place at Wembley Stadium on 5 August 1972. The artistes appearing included Bill Haley and the Comets, Chuck Berry, Little Richard and almost everyone on the British Rock n Roll scene. It was great to see Billy performing live again and among all the other all-time greats. He looked so good in his blue satin shirt and sounded wonderful as ever. A real day to remember.

Billy also started work on his third film, 'That'll be the Day'. The film starred David Essex and Ringo Starr and gave Billy the chance to play Stormy Tempest, a bit of a villain, The film was made on location, mainly on the Isle of Wight.

The story centred mainly on the character played by David Essex, who portrayed a fairground worker with a troubled love life. A great cameo role for Billy and a highly sought after double album was released after the film, featuring all the music from it. After the release in April 1973, Billy came to my home town, Southend on Sea for the big New Year's Eve Show at the Talk of the South nightclub. Billy shared the billing with his old friend Marty Wilde. A great show and an optimistic start to 1974.

He started touring again on the Cabaret circuit, trying not to overwork on doctor's orders, but he wanted to earn enough to fund the animal sanctuary he always dreamed of. There were money worries but the love of his music and his animals kept him going. Billy also met the true love of his life, Lisa Rosen. With thousands of adoring fans and many close female friends, it was amazing that up to now, he had never met the right soul-mate. Lisa was to be the person to love and inspire him for the rest of his life.

He probably overdid things during the early seventies and by 1976 he needed more heart surgery. This time to replace the heart valves that had been repaired in the previous operation. He recovered well in the Harley Street Clinic and after about three months convalescence was feeling well enough to work again. Billy had plenty of time to think about the future, whilst recuperating, and decided that now was the time to take a break from showbiz and concentrate on his much talked about animal sanctuary. With Lisa's help he found just the right place, a remote farm in Wales. The 100 acres surrounding Rhos House in Carmarthen was just what he needed for all his rescued animals and birds. He could also breed horses here, something that he had wanted to do for years. Sheep also came with the farm and Billy would often round them up on his beloved motorcycle, they didn't seem to mind.

This break from showbiz was by no means a rest, the house needed renovating, as well as all the various ponds to be made. Billy insisted on doing a lot of the work himself, but he could work at his own pace. He was really happy here, a real dream come true. All his animals and birds could have plenty of space and he could take in more. I really believe that these were the happiest years of his life, he had the farm, his London home, and Lisa there to support him. He still kept in touch with his fans and did the occasional Cabaret date. He did of course, still keep writing songs, which always seemed an easy task for him.

The Next Phase

As the seventies drew to a close Billy started to get a little restless, he had his farm how he wanted it. Was it time to get a bit more involved in showbiz again? Encouraged by his friend, Tony Read and manager Hal Carter, he decided that this was the right time for a comeback, Billy certainly had enough material for an album, this was started in July 1981, when he first got back into the studios. All was going well until March of 1982 when he was suddenly taken ill at the farm. This was a kidney virus, which seemed very serious at the time. I remember how worried we all were, just when everything seemed to be going well for him.

Billy bounced back from this setback, determined to finish the Album. There were also TV appearances. He appeared on the Russell Harty show and on Marty Wilde's 'This is your life' programme. He was getting back into the swing of things and planned a tour for 1983. There were Cabaret dates as well and the show at the Sunnyside Inn at Northampton on 4 December 1982 was more significant than any of us could imagine. We will never know if Billy had any idea that this would be his last performance. He really appeared to enjoy himself and looked great, as ever, in his tight leather suit. He even got his Mum on stage when he sang 'It's Alright Mama'. He told me he was going to have a great Christmas and New Year, then finish the Album.

It haunts me to this day, that he worked late in the studio on the night January 27th 1983, finished the Album and on January 28th he died. The news left all of us completely numb. He died at his London home in St John's Wood and the funeral took place at St John's Wood Church on 4th of February 1983.

A day I will never forget, the floral tributes laid outside the Church and people who had known each other for years, waited in silence to go into the service. Family, friends, fans and celebrities all gathered for what was a beautiful service. But the playing of Billy's song 'I'm Lost Without You' was too poignant to bear. Billy is buried in a lovely peaceful spot in London's Mill Hill Cemetery. The grave decorated with a dove and pictures of Billy, has become a quite meeting place for fans, several times a year. Or if a lone visit is preferred, there is a seat dedicated to his memory.

Not the End of the Story

After Billy's death there were many tributes, including the 'Unforgettable' TV programme. Ill timed for many of us, as it was shown the night before the funeral. In the following months, as we all tried to get on with life, the Album was released entitled 'The One and Only', and dedicated to Lisa and Tony, who had encouraged him back into the studio. In July 1983 the single 'Forget Him' was released, his last recorded work, a beautiful song, but ineptly titled, because none of us ever will forget him.

After about six months of complete emptiness, I started to come to terms with all that had happened. Billy had always said that he didn't expect to live beyond thirty, so I suppose to live to forty two was, in some way, a bonus. I truly believe, the last seven or eight years of his life were the happiest. He had achieved so much and found happiness with Lisa. He also left us so much great music and films to remember him by. The main thing now was to make sure his name was kept alive and his music heard by younger pop fans.

The fan club has done a great job over the years, not only keeping us in touch with each other, but has gained members, too young to have seen him live, but who have grown to love his music. Most of his music has been transferred to CD's and is available in most music shops. The fan club also arranges get-to-gethers of all kinds and produce a great Newsletter three or four times a year, with news of pen-friends, tribute shows, CD and souvenirs etcetera.

A major project is also to collect enough money to erect a bronze statue of Billy in his home city of Liverpool. This is, of course, a very expensive project, but at the time of writing we are well on the way to our goal. Some of Billy's friends, such as Marty Wilde and Bobby Vee, include tributes to him in their shows. There are also people who do tribute shows, such as Paul Neon and Colin Gold, all of this helps to keep Billy's memory alive.

In my opinion the best tribute shows have been by Billy's brother, Albie Wycherley, a singer in his own right and also known as Jason Eddie. His song, 'I Never Knew Colette' dedicated to Billy, is wonderful, written with true sentiment. Billy's Mum Jean, also gets involved with various events and is always happy to talk about Billy to fans.

Lisa started the Billy Fury Memorial Fund, which over the years has collected a lot of money for Heart Charities. Although Lisa has preferred to get on with her life in private, she is involved in a plan to produce a film of Billy's life, which is an exciting prospect.

Personal Memories

Having known Billy since I was just seven years old, he probably was the greatest influence in my life. We also had so much in common, our love of animals, especially horses, cars, the countryside and of course, music. I have so many happy memories, they far outweigh the sad and worrying times.

I don't know if the pop scene is as exciting for teenagers today, but it was the excitement of what to wear for shows, what Billy would wear, what he would sing, so much anticipation. Looking forward to 'Fury Monthly' magazine, reading all the pop press and waiting for the next record release. There were also letters to DJs making sure they were playing Billy's latest record on their programmes. I also remember listening to Radio Luxembourg, late at night, hoping to hear Billy's songs, not easy, as many people will remember, the sound used to keep fading and then returning, usually at the wrong moment.

Fan Club parties and picnics were great too, Billy always enjoyed get-togethers, and the presents we bought him. I also have great memories of visiting Billy on the set of 'I've Gotta Horse', of him singing to me on Yarmouth beach, tea at Fortnum and Mason's and joining him on a bird watching trip. We had great discussions on horses and dogs, he was and still is my inspiration. I still miss being able to tell him my bits of news, and him often saying, don't worry about me. Now, I just try to get on with life and get as much out of it as possible, as Billy taught me how precious every day is.

In Conclusion

If Billy sometimes drove too fast, spent money he didn't really have and worked when he wasn't well enough, it was to get as much out of life as possible. A life he knew would be short, but he left us so much.

Most of Billy's original vinyl records are now in treasured collections and you are very lucky to find many for sale. It's lucky, therefore, that so much material is now available on CDs. Some to look out for:-

The 40th Anniversary Anthology on Deran, a great double CD with a lovely write up

Paradise on Spectrum, fourteen great tracks, a personal favourite of mine

Billy Fury – The Collection Castle Comm, a good mixture of his well known hits and some rarer tracks

The Very Best of Billy Fury Hallmark, Halfway to Paradise and most of his sixties hits

We Want Billy/Billy BGO, Two great albums on one CD (one for the collector)

The Sound of Fury Decca, A great double CD with some of Billy's lesser known songs

Billy Fury – Wondrous Place Live Oz Records, this is lovely, featuring some early demo tracks, only recently discovered. Billy can be heard talking about the songs he had written. Very special, there are others too.

When I said his record 'Halfway to Paradise' summed up his life, as you will now realise, he had the talent, the looks but not the health for a long life. This has been my personal tribute to a dear friend. Dedicated to everyone who loved Billy Fury – The Singer and Ronald Wycherley – the real person. Thank you to Tony Read and the Sound of Fury Fan Club, Chris Eley, Clare Mehmet-Nugent and Sue Osborne.

Copyright of this chapter Marion Lucy Cave 8 March 2011

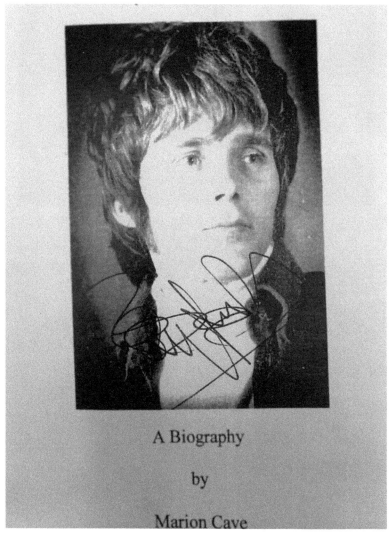

A Biography

by

Marion Cave

The front cover of Marion's book

Marion used this picture inside her book as Black/White

This is a better quality picture

Another picture that Marion used in her book

22: MARTY WILDE

Dear Michael
As requested, a personal story about Billy which has never been shared previously.
Kind wishes Marty

I knew Billy from the very beginning of his great career, when a shy young Liverpool lad came backstage to play me some songs he had written that he thought might be suitable for me to record. I listened, and immediately heard a song called 'Maybe Tomorrow' that I knew was a hit the moment I heard it. I, then heard another song that would obviously be snatched up by any publisher in the country. I told Billy that he must record these songs himself, and not to give them to anyone else. Being a songwriter, I personally couldn't have lived with the guilt of taking this man's natural gift away from him.

This simple gesture forged a friendship that would remain until his untimely death. Through the years we spent such a lot of time together, touring in the Larry Parne's Rock n Roll shows, and then later on in our careers, in the 70s, spending weekends at my home, talking and playing songs, till dawn sometimes.

One night a phone call came in to our house at around about 3am..... my wife took the call, and I told her to tell whoever it was to go and jump in the river, or words to that effect. It's Billy she said, and he's very ill. Joyce, being the caring soul she is, got a private car to bring him to our home immediately, and for the next two days Billy stayed in the small guest room at the end of our house. He spent some of the time with us and some on his own, walking into the forest opposite, peacefully studying the wildlife and returning to tell me of the wonderful birds he had seen. He had done this many times over the years when he visited our home, and was a keen and talented ornithologist, wearing his wellies, and carrying field glasses, and sometimes disappearing for hours, and always returning with a happy smiling face. On embracing my friend as we said goodbye, I knew that something was wrong...terribly wrong...as he was now so thin, and seemed so vulnerable, but I put it to the back of my mind as he smiled through the rear car window as it slowly drove away.

That wasn't to be the last time I saw Billy, as he appeared a short time later in my 'This Is Your Life' television show on the 8th of December 1982. He had become visibly thinner and when one sees the photograph of us together at that show, it was obvious to all of us who knew him that he was desperately ill – and sadly that was to be the last time we would be together.

There is a little footnote from Marty's wife, Joyce, who sent this message to me.

Thank you, Michael, My own personal sad memory was when we arrived at the airport coming back from Midem (in the south of France) with Kim – someone from the press broke the news to us. We had been due to have dinner together on our return and we were all devastated. He is sadly missed by all my family having spent so much time together. I hope all goes well with your book.

Kind regards, Joy

When Marty was in the 'Larry Parnes Mammoth Star Show 1962'

A more recent picture of Marty

This is Your Life, Marty Wilde, included Billy Fury looking very poorly

23: Maureen Spurr

My name is Maureen, I am 77 years of age as I write in November 2020. I've loved Billy Fury since I was 13/14 years old when I heard him sing 'Maybe Tomorrow'. This is and has been my all time favourite and will be played at my funeral. All those years ago I started collecting any photos I could lay my hands on and these were quickly pasted to my bedroom wall. I enjoy making montage and pencil drawings of Billy.

The heart problem that Billy had is the same as I have. I was lucky and had a Homograft replacement surgery operation and am still going strong. The operation was performed at The Royal Brompton Hospital in London. I was in theatre for over seven hours. A week later I was on the train at Euston with a change of trains at Preston, then on to Blackpool. I was in a wheel chair for the transport between stops. Although quite scary I was a lot better than I had been and it is now 17 years since the operation. If only Billy could have had this, but the developments in medical science have happened since his unfortunate experiences.

My one regret in life is that I never met Billy nor managed to go to any of his concerts. I have a son who lives in Lancaster and you have my permission to include any of my drawings and pictures in your book Michael.

The statue before it was moved to the dockside

With the dockside buildings in the background

Maureen used this for her pencil sketch

This picture gave me the idea for the book cover

24: MICHAEL HUSBAND

First of all I must explain that I am dictating this story to my sister Sue Widdowfield who is writing it down for me because I am blind.

I have been a Billy Fan from the time I heard the wonderful song 'Maybe Tomorrow' which was written by Billy. 'A Thousand Stars' also had a huge impact on me. The family consisted of mother, father, three boys, John, me, Robert and one sister named Sue. We lived at 63 Milespit Hill, opposite Mill Hill Cemetery the eventual grave of Billy Fury.

From about 1963 I became one of the people helping with a fan club under the auspices of Larry Parnes, I can remember that one of the other helpers was Ros Fleetwood

I helped with the Billy Fury Monthly Magazine. Fans would get in touch with me trying to get photos and records, particularly the rare ones, and any information about Billy, including where he was appearing, and forthcoming shows. Vera McCann (Larry Parnes Secretary), was particularly helpful, and I used to go to Derwent House (Larry's London office) to see her. She would provide all the data about Billy.

In May 1965 while I was working as a projectionist at the ABC Edgware, we had a request to help out at the Harrow ABC Theatre, where Billy was performing for one night. Of course, I happily volunteered and this gave me the opportunity to meet him for the first time. I told him I was a big fan, he asked if I had all his records. I had to admit that there was one single that I didn't have. That song was the beautiful 'My Christmas Prayer'. Billy said he would look into it but even he could not get a copy. It didn't help that the BBC banned it because of religious connotations, they were very archaic in those days.

In June 1965, when I was at Derwent House seeing Vera, she introduced me to Larry Parnes. The meeting went well, and Larry arranged for me to go to Great Yarmouth to see Billy at the Royal Aquarium Theatre which Larry owned. I went to Great Yarmouth a few times to see the Billy Fury shows. While talking back stage to Larry, the subject of my Christmas Prayer came up and he promised to arrange for a demonstration disc to be made for me. He kept to his word, and I became the proud owner of a Demo Disc made for me personally.

One subject that attracted interest from the fans was Billy appearing in the pantomime Aladdin at the New Theatre Oxford at Christmas 1965 those who got to see him were lucky because he had to withdraw part way through the run (on 14 January) due to a throat infection. Billy brought out a new EP with 'The Gamblers' including songs from the Pantomime including 'Turn your Lamp Down Low', 'I'm Saved', 'You Got Me Dizzy' and 'I Can Feel It'. This was his last recording for Decca, before moving to Parlophone.

In 1970 I went to work for London Underground and after training became a driver working on the Northern line. My younger sister Sue became a Billy fan after hearing him sing 'That's Love' and the family went to a Billy concert at the Beck Theatre, Hayes, Middlesex in 1982 when he was making a comeback. At the end of the show he was signing autographs but a theatre officer came up and asked us to disperse because Billy was not well.

A few weeks later we found that Billy was to perform at Baileys in Watford. There was a public telephone box at Morden underground station, the southern end of the Northern line. One evening, I used the phone there, on my driver break time, to book tickets. When the lady answered I was shocked to hear the show was cancelled, they had received news that Billy had died that day, of course the date was 28 January 1983.

Ironically a tribute concert was arranged to take place at the Beck Theatre, Hayes, where we had last seen Billy. We managed to get tickets and it was an emotional occasion. The performers were Marty Wilde and his daughter Kim, Joe Brown, Alvin Stardust, Dave Berry, Helen Shapiro, John Miles and a few others. They all performed without charge and the money raised was donated to the Billy Fury Memorial Fund for research into heart disease.

Personal tragedy struck me in 1990 because I suffered severed optic nerves in both eyes and became totally blind. In April 2016 Sue escorted me to the Shaw Theatre at St Pancras for a matinee performance of Michael Parkinson's Billy Fury Dance Show. We both enjoyed it so much that we went to the evening performance as well. I could hear the dialogue, the Billy recordings and could sense the reaction of the audience, Sue told me how good the dancers were. We spoke to Joan and Michael Parkinson in the interval of the first show and told them how much we were enjoying it.

This picture of Michael and Billy was taken in the dressing room at the Royal Aquarium Theatre, Great Yarmouth on 3 August 1965.

Billy and Cheryl Kennedy performed in the Pantomime Aladdin at the New Theatre Oxford, Christmas 1965 Picture used with permission of Sara Bielecki

Sue and Michael at a Mill Hill event. Michael was a driver on the London Underground Northern Line for 20 years

Thank you to Chris Eley for the picture

25: Myra Love

My story starts when I was 12 years old and I had just lost my mum to cancer. Not long after that, my dad met another woman who didn't want to take me on. I was moved from the family home in Ramsgate and put into a house with foster parents at Belvedere in Kent. It was a very dark time in my life, I had no family and no one who really cared for me.

One day, about a year later, a school friend asked me to tea after school and I stayed for the evening. We were watching television and there was a play on called 'Strictly for Sparrows'. I saw this young man in the background, sitting and strumming his guitar, singing the most beautiful song I had ever heard. He was also the most gorgeous man I had ever seen! I was smitten! I was just 13 years old and I couldn't forget him. The next time I saw him was on 'Oh Boy' one evening, I couldn't believe it, that this was the man I had seen in the play and I was mesmerised. Up till then I hadn't seen much television, my foster parents wouldn't let me sit with them to watch it. They only had one set in the house in those days, so I used to go to my friend's to watch the pop shows.

I learned his name was Billy Fury and from that moment my life took on a different meaning. I had something to cling to and of course every time he was on television my friend let me watch it at her house. Sadly, I never got to meet or even see Billy, I couldn't afford to buy a ticket to a show then. I even borrowed the money from my friend to buy his first record 'Maybe Tomorrow', it has always been my favourite to this day. I paid her back at two pence a week!

Billy came into my life when I was in a bad place and I was just a child really, he was my saviour and I will always love him and his music. He was a very special person and I will always be grateful that he came into my life when he did.

Before leaving school I did after school and weekend work in the hairdresser's that my foster parents owned, some shampooing, sweeping up and making tea etcetera. Then, when I left school at fifteen I worked there full time but did not receive a wage, just tips. It gave me a bit of pocket money but not much, anyway, I had to give half my tips to my foster parents to help pay for my keep. My father never contributed a penny towards my keep so I didn't ever have much money left over for magazines or records etcetera. I relied on friends to supply me with any magazines or newspaper cuttings of Billy. Anything at all was gratefully received! I gathered as much information as possible about Billy by reading the magazines and anything in the newspapers.

I was sixteen in 1961 when I started my hairdressing apprenticeship at a different place. My foster parents had moved away and I had to stay with a friend for a few months until I could find somewhere permanent, My foster parents couldn't take me with them as their son's marriage had broken down and they had to take in their grandchild, so no room for me. I think that if it hadn't been for Billy in my life I would have given up although I did have some very good friends. After about six months of living with my friend and her family, I was offered a room in the house of one of my clients, the rent was cheap and she also got a hair-do thrown in every week! But it still didn't leave me with much for going out etcetera. I heard all about the shows Billy was doing and would have so dearly have loved to go to see him, but it was out of the question, much to my bitter disappointment.

By this time my friend had a steady boyfriend, we were both seventeen and I had just broken up with my boyfriend so she got me a date with her boyfriend's mate. His name was Billy! We got on very well and I thought at last I might be able to and see Billy (Fury) in a show if my boy friend would take me, but it turned out he hated him, but I did not realise to what extent. As time went on it got worse, I wasn't allowed to talk about him and I had to hide all my Billy Fury stuff, (not that I had a lot) from him.

On my eighteenth birthday two friends bought me a ticket to see Billy at the local ABC Cinema in Bexleyheath, we were all going, but I swore them to secrecy because if my boyfriend found out, I was scared to think what would happen. Anyway we were in the queue waiting to go in, I was nearly sick with excitement, the one thing I wanted in the whole world was about to happen! Then one of my friends said to me Billy's just pulled up in the car, I thought she meant Billy Fury-but it was my boyfriend, somehow, and I don't know how to this day, he had found out. He jumped out of the car and got hold of my arm and pulled me out of the queue and pushed me into the car.

I was in total shock, I knew then that I would never be able to see Billy Fury, I dare not, he was very controlling and had a bad temper, so I couldn't take the risk. From that day, I just accepted my lot, as I had always done, I had no choice really, but I still had my love for Billy Fury in my heart. Up to this point I still hadn't seen or heard from my father, or my foster parents for that matter.

In 1964 Bill and I got married at Sidcup register office. I think I just felt I needed a home of my own and besides, I was pregnant. When we moved into a little one bedroom flat, my Billy mags and scrapbooks etcetera had to go with me obviously but he didn't know I had them. It was such a small flat that I had trouble hiding them, and the inevitable happened and he found them, every single thing was destroyed – my heart broke. By this time I was not even allowed to call him Billy – such was the control I had to call him Bill.

My daughter was born the following year and I doted on her. I couldn't work so my Billy stuff never got replaced as I only had enough money for the house-keeping. I had to justify every penny I spent, again, I relied on a few friends to give me newspaper cuttings and magazines when they had finished with them if they contained anything about Billy, that was the only way I could keep tabs on what was going on in the Billy world. One of them looked after my Billy things for me as I dare not have them at home. This went on for some time and I had gathered quite a collection, including a few records people had given me, which I could only play if I went to my friend's house occasionally. I had a few 'Fury Monthly' mags which I used to read over and over, and a couple of others as well. Then my friend and her husband moved down to the South coast and I had to take my Billy things home, I hid them again – but the inevitable happened and they were found. Well, that was it, no more Billy collection for me, everything was gone again.

Bill was a lorry driver and in 1972 we bought an old house in Welling which we renovated. When my eldest daughter was eight, I had my second daughter and when she was twenty-two months old my husband was killed in a road accident. I worked three jobs to keep the house going and pay the mortgage. I took on an early morning cleaning job in addition to my regular work as a hairdresser and did some private hairdressing in the evenings. In addition to looking after the children there was not time for much else.

I knew by then Billy was living on the farm in Wales, but never really heard much about him, but I still loved him and heard an occasional song on the radio. I remember seeing him in an interview just after his heart operation, and I just sat in floods of tears remembering all the years I had missed. I watch that interview quite often on YouTube now, it brings back so many memories. I have assembled a nice little collection of Billy stuff, including my prize possession, a jacket that belonged to him, that I bought from another fan, which she had won in an auction and is authenticated by Billy's brother Albie. I also have a jumper that was Billy's authenticated by Chris Eley of the 'Sound of Fury Fan Club'. I will treasure them always.

I was at work when I heard of Billy's death, I was so distraught that I had to be sent home. He was just making his 'come back' and I thought at last I might be able go to a show somewhere, but it wasn't to be. I will always love Billy and his music – which I'm sure will live on, it will if we can spread the word how wonderful and amazing he was, not only as a performer, but as a person, a true animal lover like myself and a kind and gentle person.

My two daughters are adults now obviously and have families of their own, I have three grandchildren and one step grandson. Like a lot of people, I suspect I had a very tough time, although there were a few good times as well, but Billy has always been the mainstay of my life and remains to this day, the love of my life. I joined the Sound of Fury' fan club in 2017 and have been to several Billy week ends in Blackpool and Liverpool. I've also been to Billy's grave quite a few times and have been to the statue in Liverpool a few times but could not go this year (2020) because the trip was cancelled because of the virus. Fingers crossed for the next July meeting in Liverpool which I have booked for.

When Myra sent her story to me she included a letter which I think will be of interest to the readers. Here it is, *MP*

6 Nov 2020

Dear Michael

Well, here is the information you asked for. I'm very sorry about the crossings out but you told me not to worry about that, because you are just going to type it up anyway.

Obviously I have left quite a lot out, just included things that I thought might be of interest.

What I did omit to say was that I do have a couple of connections to Billy. I was born in St Mary's Paddington and my Mother died there, as did Billy. My Father came from Toxteth, in Liverpool, one mile from the Dingle where Billy lived. I only saw my Father once after he left me, but he obviously didn't want to know, so I never saw him again. I found out recently after a search in the family archives that he died in 1984.

I hope I have given you all you wanted to know, if you need anything else, just let me know and I will do my best to give you more information.

Thank you for letting me do this, I think it has helped me to come to terms with my life. I sincerely hope that the book goes well and I hope that, if you include it, that my story will be of interest to the readers.

It is just a true and honest account of how it was for me, but I know it has made me a much stronger person. I just wish I'd had the strength of character to stand up to my husband, but there you are, I was very young and didn't really know how. Thank God for Billy Fury!!!

yours sincerely Myra

Dedicated to Myra, thank you Lee Fry for your picture.

186

Myra's youngest grand-daughter

Myra's grand-son with the dog

The oldest grand-daughter

My story starts when I was 12 years old and I had just lost my mum to cancer. Not long after that, my dad met another woman who didn't want to take me on, so I was put into a foster home. It was a very dark time in my life, I had no family and no one who really cared for me.

One day about a year later a school friend asked me to tea after school and I stayed for the evening. We were watching TV. and there was a play called 'Strictly for Sparrows' on, I saw this young man in the background, sitting and strumming his guitar sing the most beautiful song I had ever heard, he wa

Mira's story was hand written on eight sheets of foolscap paper

26: PAULINE A. BARKER

I was first aware of Billy, when I was 13 and was told about him, so watched 'Top of the Pops'. As soon as I saw him, I couldn't believe it. I fell in love with him and have been the same for the rest of my life. When I started work, in Cambridge, another girl was talking about him and told me to go to the local Music Shop, Millers, and have a look for myself. Once I had started buying Billy's records, I had to get myself a record player and still have it to this day.

Around 1965, I saw that Billy was coming to Cambridge, at the Regal and made sure that I was going to get tickets. I got up around 4 in the morning, and was first in the queue which was massive by the time we got our tickets. Of course I got front row seats so was looking forward to being really close to Billy. When the day came to see him, I was so excited. I had seen the film, 'Play it Cool' where the place had been packed. Everyone was screaming, it was crazy. Of course, the same thing happened, when Billy was on stage. I knew I would have to try and remember seeing him, but I was quite disappointed because I was so far away. The front row seats, must have been more than twenty feet from the stage, with the orchestra pit in between. I can remember more about Karl Denver and his group than I can about Billy. I remember though, that I had my autograph book, and gently threw it towards Billy.

After the show, we went to the University Arms Hotel, which was just over the road. We waited outside the back door of the Hotel and all started chanting Billy. Eventually, the door opened...... not Billy, but Tommy Roe. I don't think he thought much of us, because we wanted to see Billy.

I can remember going to Great Yarmouth on a coach trip. All the posters were on the pier theatre but the coach had to return home, well before Billy would come on stage. I sat, looking out of the window, as we drove away, just wishing I could stay to see him.

After we lost Billy, I thought that would be it. One day on our way to Peterborough to do some shopping, I heard about a fan club on the car radio and they read out the address. That night I sat up late, not knowing what to do, but wrote a letter to the Fan Club which was called The Fury Sound, at Watton in Norfolk. I had started the rest of my life with Billy. Alan and Carol Chapman were running the Fan Club, after Lisa had asked them to do it. Alan had been one of Billy's road managers. Carol told me a lovely story once, about she and her friend who were going to get them some tea so leaving their husbands behind with Billy, off they went. When they came back, the doormen would not let them in, they said, yeah yeah, we have heard it all before and still wouldn't let them in. Alan and Carol, told me all about Billy. How gentle and kind he was and that he would have loved to have seen me.

With joining the Fan Club, and then The Sound of Fury Fan Club, I have made so many lovely friends, as well as friends from The Billy Fury In Thoughts Of You Fan Club.

Alan Chapman told me, through our letters, where Billy's resting place is. With my husband and younger daughter, we managed to find the cemetery. I was not prepared for how I would feel. My husband and daughter discreetly walked away leaving me sobbing my heart out. I have never known emotion like that.

After a couple of years, the Fan Club decided that we would meet up, at around 1pm, on a Sunday. Frank Bull, was the one who hired the hall to meet in, and made all the arrangements and we have all met up, three times a year ever since. We don't need to talk much, because we all feel the same. We know how deep in our hearts Billy is.

So much has gone on over the years, we didn't have phones or Facebook to keep in touch but have all stuck together in our need to keep Billy's name alive. I used to write to Radio Stations all over the country each time we had our Meetings. We all knew that most people would not find it easy to be able to know what was going on with regard to Billy. We have been so honoured to get to know Jean and Albie Wycherley over the years. Really this means that they were 'looked after' by so many people, and knew what it would mean to Billy.

I have had so many co-incidences over the time, that, I know Billy (and my Dad) watch over us. I used to think, that it was a bit funny, that things happened at certain times. A song of Billy's on the car radio would suddenly come on, so many times I can't count them. Through The Fury Sound, I got to know a lady called Lynne Appleby, who I never met. She made mascots, badges, etc (costing around 50p each) and sold them to raise money for The Billy Fury Memorial Fund, (raising money for research into Heart Disease and Diabetes). With the money from the Fund, a piece of medical equipment for hospitals with a Billy plaque on them, would be bought. Lynne had the same complaint as Billy. She raised well over £30,000 for the Fund. It is still running today, but sadly we lost Lynne some years ago. I think it was around ten years or so, that I was able to sell what she made as well. One of the most popular things she made, was the 'Frustration Pencil', which had a little rhyme to go with it, they sold for 50 pence each.

Billy's singing is loved by so many people. His Mum had a beautiful voice as well. One time, we had a Remembrance Service in the Church at Salcombe Gardens, Mill Hill and the pianist didn't turn up. Jean then sang 'The Old Rugged Cross', I couldn't sing along with everyone else, because it was too emotional.

So much we have achieved with dedicated people working so hard over the years. Billy was sent to us for a purpose, to enrich our lives. Strong friendships have been formed through him. We 'feel' him all the days of our lives, I may not have met him, but every photo, fills our hearts. I love to hear other people's stories about him. God bless you Billy. xx Ronnie Wycherley xx

Pauline at the statue on the dockside at Liverpool

Pauline at the cake stall

Pauline made a donation by buying this brick

27: PETER WILLIAMS

When I was nine years of age, in 1955 my mother bought me a brand new Martini Colette guitar, it was in a very smart box and cost her eight guineas (that is £8-8 shillings in old money). I tried to learn to play by watching Bert Weedon who had a series of television programmes called Tuesday Rendezvous. He used his 'Play in a Day' guitar tuition method.

I was too poor to own a set of pitch pipes to tune the guitar, so we used the old method of picking up the phone, as the dialling tone was the 'G' note for the third string. Once you had got the third string in tune, it was easy to tune the rest of the strings. Bert Weedon passed away some time ago but was a great friend and influence. I have signed pictures with him.

One of them is featured at the end of this chapter. Bert's first big hit was 'Guitar Boogie Shuffle' in 1959. I recorded the B side as a dedication to him and it is 'Bert's Boogie'.

I'm putting my life on to my website in photos. It will take some time but Bert will be there. He introduced me to The Grand Order Of Water Rats which is a fantastic charity for performers when they are elderly.

After becoming kind of proficient, well I could play half a dozen chords, I had some first hand experience in a band called 'The Boys'. We did a religious TV show called 'Sunday Break' and played hymns in Church to Cliff Richard's music. We played at the Open Air Theatre on The Great Orme in Llandudno in 'The Alex Munro Show' at 'Happy Valley'. I loved his strap line 'If wet Town Hall'. We did not expect it to rain and on one occasion were out doors doing this programme and unfortunately my amp blew up as it got soaked. On another occasion at the Open Air Theatre in a talent show I had a Welsh singer with a really hard accent and it just didn't work with Roy Orbison's 'Blue Bayou'. I joined two different bands 'Mike the Invaders' and 'Peter Graham and the Gazelles' We named the group after The Gazelle, the pub in Anglesey where we were drinking at the time. We made a single record which was 'Still Waters Run Deep and Beautiful Dreamer'. We were pleased with it at the time but, unfortunately, I still have a copy!

We used to play at the Rhyl Pavilion, end of pier shows that were twice nightly on Saturdays. One time we performed with singer/guitarist Heinz Burt whose backing band didn't turn up. Heinz later became a member of 'The Tornados' Billy Fury's backing group. Then the same thing happened with the Kalin Twins, who later recorded on the Decca label and achieved success with their recordings 'When' and 'I'm Gonna Knock on Your Door'. It was a great experience for us to meet and work with these icons of the day and they received a great reception from the crowd.

I was then fortunate, around November 1962, to see Billy Fury with the Tornados at the Odeon in Llandudno, North Wales, close to where I lived in Colwyn Bay. 'What a bill, what a night'. It was just fantastic and it only seems like yesterday. I have been a fan of Billy Fury ever since. Well, I was completely knocked out by his performance. I instantly became a fan. I have never heard a chant like it from the audience. They were all screaming 'We want Billy', over, and over again. After this incredible experience, I was always at the local record shop with my six shillings and four pence when each new Billy Fury disc was released. I just loved those 'B' sides.

What was really great was the lead singer in our band was able to do a good impersonation of Billy, which meant of course we were able to play some of Billy's songs in our set. The next problem was to get the hair right. Billy looked so fantastic with his hair style, very similar to Edd Byrnes who played Kookie in '77 Sunset Strip'. In those days the barbers used to have something that looked like a form of white glue to plaster over your hair so that you could create that special quiff that Billy had, and it used to set really hard to keep your hair in place.

I am an emotional musician which makes Billy's ballads perfect for me to play. I love the sad songs and I try to put that emotional quality in my playing. Steve Etherington, John Leyton's manager, coined the phrase 'My Voice Is My Guitar', which has since become my 'strap line', the reason being I play the melody line on each of my tracks, which replaces where the vocal line would be. So may I suggest in Billy's words 'Stick Around', and look into those 'Magic Eyes', and remember, he suggested it was 'Once Upon A Dream', but please don't get 'Sleepless Nights' and 'Give Me Your Word' that 'I Will' never 'Forget Him'.

Back in the 1980s I listened to Radio Luxembourg and Radio Caroline, enjoying the new sounds coming from The Shadows. I wanted that sound, 'badly', but gave up playing for some years after this because of the day job. Then the 'Bug' came back, after meeting Alan Rondeau, a local song-writer, in Milton Keynes. I learned his material and climbed up into his loft to record his

'Shadows' style songs on a 4 track recorder. This got me into the business all over again. Then, I had a chance meeting with Big George, a presenter on BBC Three Counties Radio. He told me that I should get back out there gigging and as a result I formed a duo with Joe Price which we called 'Cool Shadow'. We worked clubs all over the place, and have been incredibly successful over the past few years doing 60's stuff and Shadows instrumentals.

I recorded my first guitar instrumental CD and thanks to Geoffrey Strachen, who re-programmed the Zoom 508 Delay Pedal, I was able to get the true sound of The Shadows so I could start recording again.

The first CD was called 'Memories'. For some reason 'The Fields of Athenry' has become part of my life. I am always asked to play it, everywhere I perform, a great Irish tune, with a strong melody line. The second CD came about as a challenge from the guys in the pub, each Sunday, someone would suggest a track. I would learn and record it. That is why my second CD is called 'Sunday Nights Inn'. My third CD came as a wonderful surprise. I had been talking to Todd Slaughter, who runs The Official Elvis Presley Fan Club. I had discussed the idea of doing an instrumental CD of Elvis' songs. So I sent him a copy of my version of 'Can't Help Falling In Love' and he loved it. Then, on Christmas Eve, I had a Christmas card from Todd saying let's do the CD. You can imagine how thrilled I was to be asked to do this tribute to Elvis. The CD is called Sentimental Me – Instrumentally Elvis.

Then came along Chris Eley of 'The Sound of Fury – The Official Billy Fury Fan Club. After some discussions, we agreed that I should do for them a tribute to Billy. This was a great success and very enjoyable to do, as Billy was always my hero. The CD is called, Remembering Billy Fury, a '2 on 1' CD plus 6 bonus tracks especially recorded for that CD.

Whilst I was recording the Billy Fury Tribute CD, I was asked to go on Radio Caroline on Dell Richardson's 'Good Rockin Tonight' I was thrilled to bits, because Radio Caroline has been THE influence on music radio in this country. Every government tried to ban this radio station, but they won through and are still going strong, based at the Maidstone TV studios, available on the Internet and Sky TV. When I did this show, Steve Etherington who manages John Leyton was listening. After a discussion we agreed that I would do an instrumental tribute to John Leyton. John is on the cover with me, and if you look closely you can see we are in 'Stitches'. The reason was, just at that moment an old war time plane was struggling to fly over us and I started humming the theme to The Great Escape, which of course was one of John's films. I then recorded my tribute CD to John, Johnny Remember Me.

What followed next was From the Vaults – Especially For You, Volume One. I discovered I had lots of tracks I had recorded over the years and I thought I would take them out of my 'Vaults' and release them. This turned out to be a very successful CD, so I then deliberately recorded another selection of tracks and released Reflections Especially For You, Volume Two.

It was suggested to me that it would be a good idea to digitally re-master my Billy Fury tracks. This sounded good to me but I wanted to give the album additional value, so I have recorded 6 bonus tracks to make a 32 track CD lasting almost 80 minutes, giving real value for money, and a celebration of our very first rock star in the UK. I have to thank Chris Eley from 'The Sound Of Fury' fan club for his help and enthusiasm for this CD. Chris' contribution is invaluable in creating the nostalgic booklet inside the CD with some wonderful photographs of Billy.

In our duo 'Cool Shadow' I played a lot of Billy's songs as instrumentals. They all went down well. Great to dance to. I always included a tribute to 'The Shadows' in our set which is my style of guitar playing, and I included some of Billy's songs in that set. We were always out performing three nights a week in pubs and clubs, so I was helping to keep Billy's music alive. These days I record guitar instrumental CDs and I have 22 titles available, which I sell on my website and on Ebay. I have the backing tracks especially made for me and try to get as close to the original music as is possible.

I am retired now but concentrate on recording instrumental CDs. The one thing guitarists always ask is what guitars do you play? My answer is:- My main guitar is a Fender Mexico. It has recorded most of the 22 CDs I have available. It was made in 1998 in Ensenada Factory, Mexico. I have owned it since it was made. It was sourced for me by a senior member of staff at Fender Guitars. I also have a Burns Marvin scroll neck guitar which was selected for me by Barry Gibson at Burns Guitars and it has a special number, as the first 50 were numbered. My website is www.peterwilliamsguitar.co.uk

A reminder of happy days back in 1968

Music and sunshine at the foot of the Great Orme

This CD will be of interest to many Billy Fury fans

The contents list

Peter is proud of this picture signed by Bert Weeden

With guitar teacher Bert Weedon, wearing the guitar that played all his hits and everyone else's too, I'm told.

28: Robert McDougall

Although his recordings and performances are legendary and universally recognised now, I first met Ronald Wycherley in Bootle's dockland at Langton Dock. It was around 1957, I was a timber ship unloader and stacker for Proctor Timber Merchants in Strand Road, Bootle and lived in Bootle Dockyard.

Billy's tugboat Formby often hauled Baltic loaded timber ships into Langton Dock, also other ships in other docks. When our timber crew quayside waited for the incoming ships to berth I noticed this tall lanky lad with sleeves rolled up perambulating fore and aft on Formby's deck, handling an assortment of tow ropes in a most athletic manner.

Later, when the tug towed ships berth settled and we waited for the ship's crew to winch timber to the quayside, Ronnie would sometimes sprint to the quayside from his also berthed tug and joke with us as we got ready to timber stack. I remember Ronnie telling me 'If you lads ever want to ship out there's vacancies on Cunard Liners and Kyle Freighters as uncertified crew'. We often sat during lunch breaks on the river wall where Ron showed me a batch of songs he had written. I took his advice and sailed to Ireland, Spain and Portugal on the Kyliefirth, a battered freighter carrying coal, sulphate, and other cargoes.

I got thrown into jail in Lisbon when I accompanied Harrison Line Liverpool sailors to Lisbon's red light district. They brawled with Lisbon toughs in the Lusitania and Mauritania clubs which they wrecked in the process. The Harrison line lads ran off. I was blind drunk and legless when the military regime and cops arrived, they blamed me for the damage to the clubs. The British Embassy got me freed after three days which included a Lisbon soldier using me for pot shot practice. I was exiled from the Merchant Navy when our ship sailed back to Liverpool, following which I did National Service in the Irish Guards.

Later, in early March 1960 I saw a photo of Billy Fury in a musical paper and recognised it as the friendly Scouser I had met in Liverpool docks. The article stated that Billy was to appear in a stage show at the Liverpool Empire with Joe Brown and two American big stars, Gene Vincent and Eddie Cochran. I went to the Empire stage door and asked for Billy who came down and recognised me immediately and invited me in. We went up two flights of stairs to the star's dressing rooms which faced the rear of the old Lime Street railway station.

Billy introduced me to Gene Vincent and Eddie Cochran who were sipping coke and whisky waiting for their afternoon sound check, also smoking cannabis. They appeared tipsy but were pleasant to me. Billy told them that I was his dockside pal and Cochran said, 'Hi-ya Buddy, join the fun' and offered me a drink, but I chose a can of beer from the table nearby. I spent some time in the company of Billy before he got a taxi to his parent's house for a rest before the show.

Next time I saw Billy was May 1960 (I think), at a Rock n Roll concert in the old Liverpool Stadium, it was a Tribute to Eddie Cochran Memorial event. Eddie had been killed in a car crash at Chippenham, on 17 April 1960. I became a photographer and years later photographed David Harman who became Dave of the group 'Dave, Dee, Dozy, Beaky Mick and Tich'. He told me that as a Wiltshire police cadet in 1960, he had attended the accident which claimed the life of Eddie Cochran. He told me the sight of Cochrane laying bloody in the road always haunted him and made him very depressed.

I saw Billy again in 1965 on Kensington High Street, London, I then lived at Palace Gate, Kensington and was working as a Security Officer at the British Museum. We greeted each other like old friends and Billy told me that he was buying clothing for general and stage use. We chatted for some time but this, sadly, was the last time I saw him.

Billy Fury tribute shows gained prominence and in August 1995 I went to the Manchester Palace Theatre when Liverpool actor Danny McCall (who had appeared in the TV series Brookside) played the role of Billy. I photographed Danny outside the theatre holding a large pictorial poster that I had made. This was published in the Manchester Evening News alongside a huge tribute to Billy.

The next tribute show that I attended was in 2001 at the Blackpool Opera House. Billy's brother Albert performed using the stage name Jason Eddie which seemed inappropriate to me because I thought that Jason Fury would have been better. I met Albert and Jean in April 2003 at the unveiling of Tom Murphy's magnificent bronze statue of Billy at the Liverpool Waterfront Museum of Life at the famous Pier Head. Large crowds attended the unveiling of the lifelike statue, many with tears unashamedly streaming down their faces, paid homage to the great Billy Fury.

The last time I saw Albie perform was at Southport Theatre in 2006. It was another Billy Fury tribute show and he was selling his own recordings of Billy and Elvis songs. Also appearing in that show were Liverpool's female dynamic duo The Passionettes, two beautiful young ladies who performed back up vocals to Jason. They usually appeared in lovely pink dresses and neck scarves. Later that year I attended another Billy Fury tribute show at Blackpool's North Pier Theatre, it featured Billy's backing band from the 1970s, the Tornados led by Chris Raynor and singer Colin Gold.

I met Jean again in 2011 at a Billy Fury convention at the Metropole Hotel in Blackpool. The concert was performed by Colin Paul and the Persuaders. Convention officer Margaret Cummings escorted Jean Wycherley, (now aged 90) and the officers presented her with a magnificent 90th birthday cake, it was an enjoyable occasion but I was saddened to hear that Albert was seriously ill at home.

Early in March 2011 the Blackpool Gazette published a full page spread about another Billy Fury tribute show to be held on 2 October at the Lowther Pavilion, Lytham St Annes. This show was to feature Billy Fury's recordings accompanied by local dance schools performing choreographed dance and narrators telling the story. The show was first performed at the Nottingham Arts Theatre to huge acclaim in aid of children's music therapy charity Jessie's Fund. The event was organised by Michael Parkinson (not the television interviewer) who was asking for stories about Billy Fury so I sent this story to him. I believe that the Billy Fury legend will become massively bigger as the years roll by. Eventually, no doubt, there will be a biopic movie of Billy's life and more stage shows replicating the Rock n Roll 1960s featuring Gene Vincent, Eddie Cochran with Billy to the forefront as Britains's greatest Rock n Roll star.

Robert McDougall at Mill Hill, the picture was taken in 1993

Robert and Ronald worked on Liverpool Docks as young men

LIVERPOOL SHIPPING NEWS

ISSUE NUMBER TWO JOURNAL
LIVERPOOL SHIPPING HISTORICAL SOCIETY.

WINTER 2007
EDITOR: ROBERT McDOUGALL

From dock labourer to security officer at Liverpool University and Museums.
Then photographer, writer and editor of the Liverpool Shipping News

29: Sandra Anderson

My younger sister, Alexis, has helped me to piece this story together, it did all happen a long time ago. My aunt, Vera McCann, was secretary to Larry Parnes for many years, she was my father's sister but as we live in Cardiff we did not see much of her. Vera was born in Poplar in 1915, one of six siblings, four of whom died in childhood. When I was 15, many moons ago, my dad and I went to stay with her in her London flat. It is funny how I can still remember the address, it was Flat 13, Derwent House, 57a Cromwell Road, Kensington. I was told that she was a special character and we were invited up to Larry Parnes penthouse to meet him.

That is when we met the man himself, Billy Fury, who lived in an adjacent flat. In those days I was a very shy person so I hardly opened my mouth. He asked me what I was going to do when I left school, I was so in awe of him it was a blur. Auntie Vera always called him 'her boy'. It was a fantastic opportunity and he appeared shy as well. I just wish I had been a little bit older to appreciate him a lot more though it was a day I will never forget.

Over the years we did not see Aunt Vera much as my dad was in the RAF so we were always travelling. She was very good friends with Kenny Everett who was a regular performer on radio and eventually on television in the 1960s. At the end of his shows she used to come on and do a dance. She once dressed as a Bunny Playboy and another time appeared wearing a dress covered with brass curtain rings which she had sewn on. This was because the song was called 'A Band of Gold' by Freda Payne.

She was also very friendly with Lionel Bart often saying she loved him but hated his hat, he wore it everywhere, even in restaurants. Here is one story that has withstood the test of time and that gave me an idea of how popular Vera was in the society that she mixed with. Lionel Bart spent a fair bit of time with Aunt Vera in Derwent House, where he would play the organ and compose some lines for a few of his musicals. He welcomed Vera chipping in occasionally!

It wasn't unusual for Mr Bart to invite Vera out for a meal (she told me he had proposed marriage to her several times). Knowing how flamboyant he could be, she was taking no chances when he invited her out to a London restaurant one evening as she quizzed him regarding his planned attire. He assured her that he would be appropriately dressed, wearing a suit and tie. Armed with that information Vera decided she would wear a trouser suit, one that she had made and worn on the Kenny Everett Show. He must have had an amazing sense of humour as he showed up in leather trousers, high heeled boots, a Cape and Sombrero! Vera said they entered the restaurant and the manager walked directly towards her, welcoming her with open arms but ignoring Lionel Bart as he looked on!

Vera hated leaving London and visited us in Wales, only for my dad's funeral and when mum remarried. I don't know if Lee Everett is still alive but Vera was great friends with her, in fact it was Lee who wrote to me to tell me when my Aunt Vera had died. She had passed away in her sleep sometime in 1980.

Thank you Michael for immortalising a dear and special Aunty.

The building where Larry Parnes had his penthouse apartment. Vera McCann, Billy Fury and Vince Eager also occupied flats there.

Vera (Floral dress), her sister Sandra (Turquoise) and younger sister Alexis (White) at a wedding in August 1976.

Billy Fury with Vera's dog

Tommy Steele was one of the social group

With yet another dog

Vera in Kenny Everett television show attire

A signed picture that he gave to Vera McCann

Billy with Vera, not sure who the young lady is. Thank you to Vera's son Edwin
for sending these pictures from his home in Canada

30: Vince Eager – My Pal Bill

It's not until you have the opportunity to reflect on life that the significance of certain events take on their full meaning. My first meeting with Ronald Wycherley was outside the Birkenhead Essoldo stage door in October 1958. That chance meeting, I was going for a Wimpy burger with drummer Brian Bennett when Ronnie approached me, proved to be a stellar moment. What if Ronnie had not been a determined guy, what if I had not been going out for a Wimpy, what if I had ignored his approach, what if Larry Parnes had not been in the theatre. Would Ronnie have ever become Britain's greatest Rock n Roller? I think he would. Someone with his undoubted talent eventually shows upon the show business radar.

Ronnie soon became Billy and he set off for the royal suburb of Knightsbridge in London. During the year Billy and I were flatmates we never looked upon each other as something more than flatmates. We both experienced difficult and great times together. Our bond was being away from our parents and in an alien environment. From not having two halfpennies to rub together to being lorded in high circles was all part of our experience.

A more caring, gentle or kinder person than Billy you couldn't find. Of all the stage names Larry Parnes gave his protégés, I think 'Billy Fury' was genius. Larry's choosing of boy next-door first names, such as Tommy, Marty, Billy and then second names, Steele, Wilde and Fury certainly gave the artistes something of a split personality. The off stage 'Billy' and the on stage 'Fury' were just that. You could not believe that 'Billy' could become 'Fury' but he did with consummate ease.

Billy was two different people, and one person who recognised Billy's potential was the 'Oh Boy' TV show Producer Jack Good. He presented Billy to the nation and got it spot on. There is no doubt that had it not been someone who had the skill and enthusiasm for his artistes that Jack had, then things could have turned out very differently. I was asked a few years ago if I had any suggestions as to who might be suitable to unveil Billy's statue in Liverpool. At the time I had just rekindled my friendship with Jack and he was an obvious choice. The only problem was that Jack had become a recluse and was happy to get on with his painting whilst the world 'rocked' by. After a few glasses of Lager and Merlot, Jack agreed to take on the task. Jack's acceptance was punctuated by him insisting that he would not do it for anyone other than Billy. It was Jack who first presented Billy to the nation, and it was Jack who was to present his statue to the world. Jack's actions in unveiling Billy's statue were the final seal of approval that Billy Fury was without doubt Britain's greatest Rock n Roller.

Billy and Vince busy in the kitchen

Vince Eager on stage

31: Young dancers

The day after the final performance of the Billy Fury Dance show at Nottingham Arts Theatre (see chapter 2) Maggie Andrew, the show director, suggested that I should put on some sort of party for all the people who had taken part. She suggested hiring a room somewhere, I was not keen because I had just experienced months of stress and expenditure. I discussed it with Joan who offered to put a party on at our house provided that I paid for everything.

The party happened on 14 August 2010, we got an idea of how many people would be there and I was pleased that some had to refuse because they were involved on other projects. Joan prepared a buffet and I organised some pop and booze. It was a pleasant event and everyone enjoyed it, even old scrooge me.

At around 6pm three of the youngest performers said that they wanted to put a little show on themselves and asked if there was somewhere they could do it. I could only suggest the garage but told them that it had a concrete floor. Maggie, who had directed the show, immediately said she would like to help but the girls said they wanted to do it all by themselves. The parents, girls and I went to the garage and we fixed up a back cloth from a canvas sign that had advertised the show. We put some heaters on and cleared space for them. One of the girls parents had a small tape player and we rigged lights up. After that the adults were dismissed and the girls said that they would send for us when they were ready.

At around 10pm the adults were asked to go to the garage. The girls, average age twelve, whose names are Fabiane Leame, Sky Fletcher and Erin Keogh asked one of the mothers to operate the tape player. They told us they had choreographed routines to two Billy Fury songs. They and their parents gave me permission to video so in the strange surroundings of the garage the show went ahead.

The quality of sound and light was appalling but the performance accompanied by much laughter and giggling was lovely. They chose Billy Fury singing 'Turn your Lamp Down Low' and 'Run to my Loving Arms' as the songs to dance to. In preparation for this book I loaded the video to my YouTube channel name Michael notthatone Parkinson with the title 'Young dancers have fun to Billy Fury Songs, Nottingham after show party'. If you have access to YouTube you can view the video. I am proud that my shows get young people to know about the Billy Fury songs and backing tracks and this is a perfect example.

A rather blurred picture from the YouTube video

Skye Fletcher as she looks in 2021

32: NOT THE END

This is the final chapter in the book but not the final chapter in the Billy Fury story. It is now 63 years since young Ronald Wycherley was pushed on stage at the Essoldo, Liverpool after that amazing interview. His music is still being listened to and YouTube has many video clips showing all aspects of his life, songs and achievements. During the last few days another milestone in his history has passed in amazing circumstances because of the Covid19 pandemic that is affecting the whole planet.

The 28th of January 2021 was the 38th anniversary of the death of Billy Fury but the recently refurbished grave at Mill Hill Cemetery in North London was strangely bare because travel restrictions did not allow people to travel. It was obvious that I would not be able to use my train tickets for travel from my home in Nottinghamshire in order to do the planned graveside tribute as a finale to this book. A lady by the name of Sue Widdowfield, who I had met at the grave previously, agreed to travel the short distance from her home to the grave so that she could send pictures enabling me to formulate a tribute at home.

I used the pictures and video of my Nottingham Billy Fury dance show, performed in 2010, to make the tribute and include the words and songs used here:-

Narrator

On 28 January 1983, Billy or to be precise, Ronald Wycherley, was found unconscious. He was taken from his apartment and was pronounced dead on arrival at St Mary's Hospital, Paddington. The heart weakness that had dogged him all his life finally claimed him. He was 42 years old. Our choir will sing Psalm 23. This was used in the funeral service at St John's Wood Church, London.

All members of the cast sang the first three verses of Psalm 23, tune, Crimond

The Lord's my Shepherd, I'll not want,
He makes me down to lie
In Pastures green; He leadeth me
The quiet waters by.

My soul he doth restore again
And me to walk doth make
Within the paths of righteousness
E'en for his own name's sake

Yea, though I walk in death's dark veil,
Yet will I fear no ill;
For thou art with me and my rod
And staff me comfort still

This was immediately followed by the speaking voice of Billy narrating words he had written himself:-
They walked on the beach at dawn, a deserted place closer to life,
They ran and smiled at the sea and the sky, breathing in a world of their own,
It mattered little the shifting of sand, the glory and promises enchanting our land
They are as the birds on the wing and thinking of sleep,
Somewhere warm and somewhere dry, a world of their own
A something somewhere, up high, where they are soaring, never to die

This was immediately followed by Billy singing 'Forget Him' accompanied by solo dance from Cora Vanaman

Narrator

Ironically both Billy Fury and Elvis Presley died at the same age of 42.

Billy left a legacy of over 340 recordings. He was in the singles' charts for 281 weeks and the album charts for 51 weeks. He had a career total of 29 hit singles and 11 top ten hits. His recording are regularly played on Radio and his films are being watched and sold today. He is buried in Paddington Cemetery Mill Hill, North London. The grave is frequently visited and maintained by fans. The headstone bears the inscription, 'His Music Gave Pleasure to Millions' . Here we are 27 years later (the show was in 2010), listening to his unique voice and those lovely songs, many written by Billy himself. A bronze statue stands on the riverside at Liverpool. It features Billy looking out over the Mersey where he used to work on a tugboat. It took the Sound of Fury Fan Club six years and four months to raise over forty thousand pounds for the statue. The inscription on the plaque reads:-

Billy Fury (Ronald Wycherley)
17 April 1940 to 28 January 1983
Legendary British Rock n Roll star
Major UK Chart Artist
Outstanding and Charismatic Live Performer
Songwriter, Animal Lover and Gentle Man
This statue has been achieved through the dedication of Billy Fury Fans
Worldwide
Sculptured by fellow Liverpudlian Tom Murphy
These words are a lasting monument to Billy Fury

This was followed by Billy singing 'Devil or Angel' accompanied by dance from six members of the cast.

This tribute is on YouTube with the title:-

Billy Fury Tribute 28 Jan 2021, Nottingham Arts Theatre Dancers

The reason I believe that Billy Fury will be popular for many years to come is that younger people will discover his singing voice, clear diction, good looks and be impressed that he was Britain's first Rock n Roller. I am sure that new stories will emerge similar to what you have read in this book. There will be tribute singers performing his songs, guitarists will be inspired to play his melodies or people will be inspired by a particular song. Perhaps there will be someone, like me, or dance schools, who will promote shows with dancers performing to Billy Fury songs.

Thank you for reading my book and I sincerely hope that you have enjoyed it.

Michael Parkinson

Picture courtesy of Lee Fry

You Tube Channel

My YouTube channel name is
Michael notthatone Parkinson

Other titles from Michael Parkinson

From Billy Fury to YouTube ISBN 978-1-78222-588-1

Ovaltineys to Sheredean Girls Club ISBN 978-1-78222-675-8

Thames Path Walk ISBN 978-1-78222-755-7